Symbols Around Us

Symbols
Around Us

Sven Tito Achen

VNR **VAN NOSTRAND REINHOLD COMPANY**
NEW YORK   CINCINNATI   TORONTO   LONDON   MELBOURNE

Translated from the Danish by Reginald Spink
Printed in the United States of America
Designed by Loudan Enterprise

Published in 1978 by Van Nostrand Reinhold Company
A division of Litton Educational Publishing, Inc.
135 West 50th Street, New York, NY 10020, U.S.A.

Van Nostrand Reinhold Limited
1410 Birchmount Road, Scarborough, Ontario M1P 2E7, Canada

Van Nostrand Reinhold Australia Pty. Limited
17 Queen Street, Mitcham, Victòria 3132, Australia

Van Nostrand Reinhold Company Limited
Molly Millars Lane, Wokingham, Berkshire, England

16 15 14 13 12 11 10 9 8 7 6 5 4 3 2 1

Library of Congress Cataloging in Publication Data
Achen, Sven Tito.
    Symbols around us.
    Translation of Symboler omkring os.
    Includes index.
    1. Symbolism. 2. Signs and symbols. I. Title.
CB475.A2313   111   77-17356
ISBN 0-442-20251-2

Contents

What is a Symbol?

In July 1955 President Eisenhower met Prime Minister Bulganin of Russia in Geneva. The object was to put an end to the Cold War, and the conference was anticipated with great hopes of detente and a reduction of armaments. When the president flew in to Washington after the conference, it was pouring with rain. An airport official stood ready with an umbrella but was brushed aside by one of Eisenhower's aides, and the President got soaked before he reached shelter.

Why did he not want to be protected from the rain? Because he wanted at all costs to avoid any pictures connected with an umbrella. Before the Second World War another democratic statesman, Neville Chamberlain, had flown to meetings with a dictator, with the results that we all know. One of the things that the world had noticed most about Chamberlain was his umbrella. It had come to be identified with him, and, because of the failure of his policies, the umbrella became a symbol of appeasement, impotence, or cowardice. So much importance was still attributed to this symbol 17 years later that it was preferable that the president of the United States get drenched than that he be photographed with an umbrella.

Symbols play a bigger part in our lives than we are normally aware of. From baptism to burial, our existence is permeated with symbolic acts; our social conventions are to a large extent symbolical and our clothing likewise. Above all we are surrounded by symbolic images. We encounter symbols everywhere, in big things and little, on billboards and in parliaments, in kindergarten and cathedral, in war and peace, in love, in art, in politics, in the newspaper, in public relations and religion, education and propaganda. The use of symbols is perhaps the most effective way to influence people. Ask the Communists—or the Roman Catholics! From prehistoric rock engravings and cave paintings to Women's Lib and ban-the-bomb demonstrations, human life and ideas have been full of symbols. People have lived for symbols, and people have sometimes gone to their death for symbols.

The 62 pictorial and other visual symbols presented in this book are all taken from everyday life. They are symbols that anyone who uses his eyes and perhaps occasionally visits a museum or church may meet. Hardly any have been treated exhaustively; more could be said of all of them. On some pictorial symbols whole books, even rows of books, have been written. Others, on the other hand, remain completely unexplored, their treatment in this book perhaps the first that they have ever been given.

The word "symbol" itself has so many connotations that it is wise to clarify the sense in which it is used in this book. The word is Greek and is far more recent than the idea. Its early history is interesting and worth retelling because it helps to provide a definition.

When two people in ancient Greece made an agreement, they often sealed it by breaking something—a tablet, a ring, a piece of pottery—into two pieces and keeping one-half each. If one of the contracting parties later wanted the bargain honored, he or his representative would identify himself by fitting his part of the broken object into the other's.

To "match" was in Greek *symballein*, and the two pieces were called *symbola*. This word gradually came to mean "recognition sign" in a wider sense, e.g. for members of a secret society or persecuted minority. The first Christians had various "symbols" by which they could identify themselves to

Symbols on a 3rd-century Christian tombstone: a "crown of glory" at the top; in the middle two fishes. The fish was one of the most popular symbols of Christianity. Between the fishes is an anchor, which might stand for hope (of resurrection) or for the safe anchorage of God.

one another without revealing anything to anybody else.

A symbol was originally a thing, a sign, or a word used for mutual recognition and with an understood "meaning." A fragment of pottery—the right fragment!—could mean, for instance, "I've come from so-and-so and want payment of a hundred drachmas." A sign—say, the outline of a fish scratched on the ground and quickly erased—might mean "I am a Christian." From this beginning and through a long succession of derivations and extensions over centuries "symbol" came to mean almost any sort of device, sign, message, or form of recognition, linguistic or nonlinguistic, intentional or unintentional. To a theologian "symbol" means "creed"; to a computer operator it may mean the holes in a data card.

Midway between these extremes lies the meaning that has been the most important and that is attached to the word here. In this book "symbol" denotes something—for example, a device or an actual thing, a flower or a color—that has a "meaning" other than its most obvious one. In particular a symbol is *a device or an image representing one thing but meaning something else.*

The symbol is understood only by the initiated, and its meaning cannot be deduced. There is no mental connection, either rational or logical, between the symbol and its meaning. One may *know* that the image of an apple symbolizes man's fall or that a horseshoe or a picture of one stands for luck. But the meaning cannot be arrived at by reasoning.

Certain symbols have become so well-known that everybody "understands" them: the cross stands for Christianity, and the swastika for Nazism. In fact, however, it is not a case of "understanding" but of previous knowledge. A person from another civilization would not be able to imagine the meaning.

A few other related terms crop up in this book.

"Allegory" in a way means the same thing as "symbol": an image representing one thing but meaning another. But there is an important difference. A symbol is simple and uncomplicated (a crescent, a hammer), and, as already stated, it is really a secret sign, unintelligible except to the initiated. An allegory is complex, sometimes extremely complicated, and is the reverse of secret. What it means should preferably be understood by everybody; it should be capable of being "read" or interpreted; everybody should be able to agree on its meaning.

Example of an allegory: two female figures beneath a lamb (not in the photograph due to the curved arch of the church). The woman on the left is blindfolded: she does not want to know the truth or does not know what she is doing. She loses her crown and her majesty. She represents Synagoga, or Jewry. With her lance she slays the lamb—Jesus—dead upon the cross. The woman on the right is crowned and can see; she represents majesty and truth. She is Ecclesia, the Christian Church. In the chalice she is collecting the blood of the lamb, the sacrificed blood of Jesus, the wine of the Christian communion. Beneath Ecclesia is the serpent of the Fall or of heresy, which she is treading underfoot. Fresco from about 1200 in Spentrup Church, Jutland, Denmark. Photo: Danish National Museum.

Example of a symbol. A rock towers above a rough sea but remains unshakable, illustrating the bearer's ideal, "unwavering and unyielding." Swedish seal, c. 1700.

An example of an allegorical figure is Justitia, the goddess of justice and law. She holds a pair of scales in one hand for weighing the evidence. She hold a sword in the other hand to punish the guilty. She is blindfolded; unable to see the parties to the case, she is impartial. The various components of an allegory may well consist of symbols, as in this example (scales, sword). A symbol is an "agreed" sign, and one can, of course, agree about anything. It follows that the same picture or image can *symbolize* very different things and indeed opposites. A lion can symbolize God as well as the Devil. A mirror can symbolize wisdom but also vanity. An allegory, on the other hand, should be intelligible to anybody and thus should have only one connotation.

Example of a pictogram. The picture of a comb and scissors clearly indicates a hairdressing salon. A pictogram has no "other meaning."

Example of an attribute. The picture is from a fresco, c. 1375, in Hillerslev Church in Denmark. It represents a woman, but who is she? The halo indicates a saint, and the crown either a virgin or royalty. But both can have many meanings. Her real attribute and identification are the forceps with a tooth that she is holding in her hand, which show her to be St. Apollania. During the persecutions of the Emperor Decius at Alexandria in 249 A.D. she was tortured by having her teeth extracted before being burned at the stake, and in ecclesiastical art she is represented as holding a forceps with a tooth. She gives protection against toothache and is the patron saint of dentists. Photo: Danish National Museum.

A "pictogram" is a fairly recent term for an old idea. A pictogram is a picture that means what it represents and represents what it means as directly and as unmistakably as possible. If a picture of a fish means "Here is a fishmonger's," it is a pictogram. If it means "I am a Christian," it is a symbol. Pictograms are becoming increasingly important in international communications (e.g., transportation, tourism, Olympic Games) and in instructions for operating, say, electronic equipment. They are often called symbols, but pictograms would be more correct.

An "attribute" is an accessory. Attributes are predetermined identification signs affixed, in visual art especially, to gods and saints but also to allegorical personifications. Examples of these are: Neptune's trident, Thor's hammer, the scales of Justice, the keys of St. Peter, and the man, lion, ox, and eagle of the four evangelists. Without their attributes it would usually be impossible to tell who was who. There are also collective attributes, such as the palm branch of martyrs and the shell of pilgrims. Some attributes have started out as symbols, which would explain why they were chosen. Others may have developed into symbols through their association with their respective god or saint and with his or her functions. Others have no symbolic significance.

"Insignias" are indications of the power or dignity of an office or a function, such as the Pope's tiara, the field marshal's baton, the chamberlain's key, or the mayor's chain. Crown, scepter, and orb are the insignias of royalty; coats of arms and national flags are state insignias. But the word "insignia" may also be employed in a wider sense to include, for example, the tailor's scissors; the dentist's forceps, drill, and mirror; the chef's ladle and cap; or the artist's brush and palette.

The borderline between these various categories is anything but sharp, however, as will be shown in the following pages. Insignias can be attributes and vice versa. Where does the symbol end and the allegory begin? Even pictograms and symbols may overlap. Furthermore, a device belonging to any of these categories may become so popular and so frequently repeated that it will lose its connotation and end up as merely an ornament. In the world of symbols, as in that of men, success is sometimes a greater hazard to character than misfortune.

Example of the use of insignia: three men in a French woodcut from the beginning of the 16th century. The man at the right is shown by his crown and scepter to be a king, and the lilies on his cloak indicate that he is the king of France. The man in the middle, with the finer, closed crown, orb, and sword of absolute power, must be the Holy Roman Emperor. The man on the left, with the triple crown and triple cross, is the Pope.

Celestial Bodies

The Crescent

One of the loveliest sights in all of nature is that of the sickle moon, the curved, nearly new crescent with its twin pointed horns. It is especially so in the South and the Orient, where days are hot and the people only come really to life after dark to breathe the cool night air on the flat rooftops of their houses.

It almost goes without saying that the beautiful crescent should have been identified with the most exalted powers in life: kings (usually together with the sun) and a variety of gods and especially goddesses. One of the latter was Hecate, the patron goddess of Byzantium, and her device was adopted by the city in its coat of arms in antiquity. Another moon goddess was Diana (Artemis to the Greeks), whose most celebrated temple was at Ephesus in Asia Minor and whom St. Paul fulminated against in chapter 19 of the Acts of the Apostles. Worship of the moon goddesses died out with the advance of Christianity, but men refused to give up the crescent as an emblem, and it was adopted by the Virgin Mary. A crescent moon became an attribute of the Queen of Heaven, the crescent in the arms of Byzantium (by then renamed Constantinople) being regarded as a Marian symbol.

The crescent as a Moslem symbol: *The arms of the Turkish emperor*, drawn
c. 1700 by an Austrian artist. The composition has been adapted to European
models, but the crescent is genuine enough.

In 1453 the Turks captured this last bastion of the Eastern
Roman Empire, the city of Constantinople itself, and the
Turkish armies advanced under banners and standards bearing a crescent, a device that some scholars believe they took
over from their vanquished enemy. This is not correct. Use of
the crescent by the Turks can be traced as far back as the 12th
century in their central Asian homeland. It was certainly their
own, and in succeeding centuries it hung, a constant threat,
over eastern and southern Europe. The very word "crescent"
became synonymous in every European language with "Turk,"
"Islam," "infidel." The picture of the Virgin Mary standing in a
crescent was now taken to mean that she was trampling the
dreaded anti-Christian foe underfoot. In 1698 the citizens of
Vienna took down the old weather vane, shaped like a

The crescent as a Christian symbol: . . . *a woman clothed with the sun and the moon ùnder her feet* (Revelation 12:1). The Virgin Mary and infant Jesus in a woodcut by Albrecht Dürer, 1511.

crescent, from the cathedral of St. Stephen. It had ceased to be regarded as a Christian symbol.

From Turkey the crescent spread to other Muslim countries, becoming almost universally the symbol of Islam. Its use has somewhat declined, however, in recent years. Egypt abolished her crescent flag and arms in 1958, and Libya hers in 1969. But the crescent still figures in the flags of a number of other countries, including Mauritania, Algeria, Tunisia, Turkey, Pakistan, and Malaysia. And it is employed as the emblem of the Muslim Red Cross. "Cross?" No! In Muslim countries the organization is called, of course, the Red Crescent.

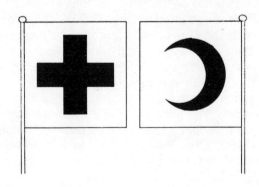

The Sun

The part of the universe that is inhabited by the human race is called the solar system, and the name is appropriate. The sun is the center and focal point of our lives. It is the sun's enormous magnet that keeps the earth and the other planets firmly on their courses. Which means, in turn, that both what we call "day" and what we call "the year," our small time scale and our large one, the starting point of nearly all human knowledge and calculation, are created by the sun.

It is the sun that gives us light and heat. All life on earth is dependent on the sun, Fertility and maturity are the sun's work. From the sun come abundance, happiness, prosperity, and beauty. It is reflected in our language: "a place in the sun," "where the sun never sets," "make hay while the sun shines," "you are my sunshine."

The sun has been worshipped all over the world by nearly every tribe of almost every religion. Sometimes it was the physical sun, the sun's disk, that was worshipped. So it must have been in Denmark, for example, in the Bronze Age, as is witnessed by the famous Sun Chariot, consisting of a sun disk drawn by a horse, now in the National Museum in Copenhagen. Elsewhere it was a sun god in human form (perhaps the driver of the sun's wagon), such as the Greek Helios and Apollo or the Persian god Mithras.

The sun of Mithras was especially vigorous. It lived on in Persia and shines today from the back of a lion in the national arms of Iran. Mithras became so popular in the Roman Empire that the government established an official cult of *Sol invictus,* "the conquering sun," a title that was subsequently adopted by the Christian Church of Christ. And our holy day set aside for worship is Sunday—that is, "the sun's day." Even the Old Testament, generally antipathetic to images, refers to the Lord God as "the Sun." The sun stood for God and God's Creation: it was an image of divinity, majesty, beauty, and goodness. It was a protector, a helper, and a cleanser.

Goodness and protection, yes—and no! In some Egyptian representations of the sun each ray ends in a caressing hand. The sun is not only a friend, however, but also an enemy, its work evident in heat, fire, drought, thirst, and death ("The sun is my undoing"). Is it in fact fear and dread that underlie much worship of the sun, at any rate in hot countries? Will it sometimes have been worshipped in order to avert its evil effects? We have the graphic word "godfearing."

Where do gods end and where do kings begin? In Babylon the king was "his realm's sun." And "Son of the Sun" was the official title of the Inca rulers of South America and the rulers of Egypt and China. The national flag of Japan incorporates the red sun disk that was the device of the old Tokugawa dynasty. When a king was portrayed, it was often as a sun: that is, with a wreath of sun rays on his head. From the Orient the custom passed to Greek and Roman rulers, and from this corona developed two widely used symbolic solar images, the halo of the saint and the crown of kings.

The halo denotes the sunbeams, the luminosity, radiating from divine or holy persons. Gods might be depicted with a

God the Father seated in heaven, his right hand raised in benediction and his head radiant like the sun. Woodcut by Albrecht Dürer, c. 1498, in his series of illustrations of Revelation.

halo as well as emperors and other outstanding men such as poets and philosophers. There are examples from classical times of Homer and Virgil represented with haloes. From the 4th century Christian artists began to show Jesus with a halo and later Mary and the apostles; in time, the halo—in the form of a surrounding nimbus or aureole—became the distinctive sign of a saint. Sometimes the beams radiated not from the head but from the whole body, which was enclosed by an aureole. This is familiar in images of Buddha and Mohammed, and in Christianity it became a special attribute of Mary, the Mother of God.

These representations were used in flat, painted pictures. In sculptures and in real life the divine rays were shaped like a frontlet or corona from which radiated sunbeams of gold, set with glittering jewels. It was from such golden-rayed frontlets that the crown developed, the Latin word for "frontlet" being *corona*. The importance that was attached to this solar symbol is indicated by the fact that the word "crown" in Europe became almost synonymous with royal power, indeed the state (the Crown in Britain). Later on in the baroque age the royal crown acquired loops that met over the brow, and the entire crown was shaped like a sort of helmet or cap. But until about 1600 royal crowns were sometimes designed with pointed rays as an image of the sun, the king's face representing the sun's disk.

To the absolutist kings the symbol of the sun expressed all that they aspired to be. It was the indication that they were God's equals, that they wielded the supreme power, and that they were the hub of society. When pleased, they allowed "the light of their countenance to shine forth." The most typical example is Louis XIV, King of France from 1643 to 1715. He was called the "Sun King," but it was not an appellation that came of itself or was given to him. The name was thought up by the king and his chief minister, Cardinal Mazarin, as a deliberate part of their policy of psychological domination. Solar images and symbols were incorporated in official decorations, in art, in military banners, in literature, on the stage, in every form of ornamentation and propaganda. The meaning was: what the sun is in the sky, Louis XIV is on earth. The other monarchs of Europe are only moons and planets.

This led to a war of symbols. The arms of Prussia consisted of an eagle, and, according to ancient popular belief, the eagle is the only creature that can bear to look straight at the sun without blinking. It was a story that the princes and kings of Prussia could use! In those years the Prussian eagle was often shown flying aggressively against a sun—a very pale sun—with a matching Latin motto: *Non soli cedit* ('It does not yield to the sun').

From God and king it was not far to "Number 1." A figure of the sun became the symbol of the best, the first, of anything that in rank, importance, or beauty surpassed everything else. For example, a sun stood for "gold," the first of metals. In Germany a small figure of the sun is the goldsmiths' standard. To alchemists a sun might stand for "man," and a moon for "woman." (Let me say that this is not my own assessment: I merely report.) Of course, this did not stop amorous males from transposing the roles.

"The selfsame sun that shines upon his court/ hides not his visage from our cottage/ but looks on alike . . ." The sun sees everything, illuminates everything, and so knows everything. It became a symbol of omniscience, insight ("as clear as daylight"), wisdom, prudence, and enlightenment. In English-speaking countries "Sun" is a common name for newspapers, *e.g.* The *Baltimore Sun*. Whoever knows everything knows the truth, and above all the sun became an image of truth, often represented as a naked women (she has nothing to hide) holding a figure of the sun.

The sun also reveals what we would rather conceal, from stains on our winter clothes to the shabbiest actions. To the Pythagorean philosophers of Greece the sun was a symbol of irrefutable evidence and a just sentence, an image later transferred to Jesus, "the Sun of Righteousness." From Jesus the solar symbol spread, coming to stand for the goodness of God and God's will, for theology and Christian virtue. A sun was the attribute of a number of saints, especially those who combined a keen intellect with sanctity, such as St. Thomas Aquinas and Ignatius Loyola, the founder of the Jesuit order. In Scandinavia, however, the sun is associated with St. David, who brought Christianity to Vestmanland in Sweden. The devout man was both shortsighted and absentminded and once hung his gloves to dry on a sunbeam instead of a peg.

A very important part of the symbolism of the sun is connected with its rise. Sunrise, a new day, meant the triumph of light, an end to the power of darkness and the night of tyranny and colonialism. It spelt the dawn of liberty and a new era for the nations. It was "the new dawn." The rising sun became a symbol of freedom, the future, and progress. When the Spanish colonies of South America rebelled against the mother country about 1810, they did so under the "banner of the sun," and a succession of new states included a rising sun in their national arms or flags, among them Argentina, Peru, Cuba, Uruguay, and Ecuador. Several of the states of North America did the same, including Arizona, Kansas, and Illinois. In 1847 liberated slaves founded their own state of Liberia ("Land of Freedom"), with a sun in its national arms. Others followed: the Philippines in 1898 and the Republic of China in 1906. When the Soviet Union included the rising sun in its arms in 1917, a new chain reaction was set in motion (the rising sun

The New World, both North and South America, adopted the sun, especially the rising sun, as a symbol of liberty and progress. A good example is the symbol of the state of Illinois. The picture dates from 1810 when Illinois was not yet a state but only a territory. In 1818 it was admitted as the 21st state to the Union, and in 1915 it placed the sun in its state flag.

figures in the arms of nearly every Soviet republic), and with the African anticolonial liberation movements another. Today a sun or sunrise is perhaps the most common device in national symbolism.

It is not, however, just the fact of the sun rising but also the way it rises. The sun is the most regular, the most predictable phenomenon we know. Its rising and setting can be calculated in advance to within seconds. And it never fails. The sun thus came to symbolize absolute reliability, the immutability of the world order as against chaos. In Latin the rising sun is called *oriens*, from which we get the word and the idea of "orientation," or the determination of one's location and direction. All over the world temples and other shrines are "oriented" to the rising sun, to the east. It is true of Christian churches to this day.

The sun also marks off the year with the recurring seasons that are among our greatest riches, the spring and autumnal equinoxes and the summer and winter solstices. The very duality of these twin poles of midsummer and midwinter and the emotional and dimensional dissonance intrinsic in each of them are the work of the sun. The joy of midsummer conceals a despair: the year has culminated, and from now on there will be decline. And in the darkness of midwinter there is hidden rejoicing: we have come to the bottom, and things will go forward toward the light and a new happiness. The midwinter sun, pale and low though it is, symbolizes a great hope, indeed an assurance, a certitude.

Paper cut by Hans Christian Andersen on a Danish Christmas seal, 1975.

The solstice is man's oldest celebration, the most fundamental. All nations celebrate the solstice, although names and motivations vary. For centuries the Church tried to eradicate this paganism but, as it did not succeed, reversed its policy and annexed the solstice. Probably in the year 354 the Church fixed the birth of Christ on December 25 and that of John the Baptist on Midsummer Day. The midwinter festival of the returning sun, the greatest feast of the year, ceased to be the Saturnalia of the Romans and the Yule of the Anglo-Saxons. It was Krist-mess, or Christmas.

The Star

The young man on the street handed me a leaflet. "Solidarity with Chile," it said, and it had been issued by the Danish Communist Party. The cover was made to look like the Chilean flag: it was divided horizontally into white and red, with a blue corner panel enclosing a five-pointed white star.

Solidarity with Chile. This star resembles the Communist stars of the Soviet Union, China, North Korea, and others, but in fact the flag of Chile is a direct descendant of the Stars and Stripes. Indeed, the Communist stars may be, too!

A similar five-pointed star was incorporated in the flags of
North Vietnam and the Vietcong and is included in the flags or
national arms of nearly every Communist country: China,
North Korea, Yugoslavia, and, above all, the Soviet Union,
which set the pattern for the rest. The five-pointed star of Chile
could clearly be regarded as another in this succession of
Communist stars.

That, however, would be a gross fallacy. Chile's star has
quite a different origin. When the 13 British colonies on the
eastern shores of North America broke away from the mother
country and, on July 4, 1776, declared themselves independent, one of the things that had to be chosen was a flag for
these "united states." Until then they had used the flag of the
United Kingdom, a red banner with the British union flag, the
Union Jack, in a corner. That, broadly speaking, is what they
continued to do. They changed only one thing: the red field
was converted into a number of horizontal red and white
stripes, an idea that they may have taken from the early flag of
the Dutch republic. The British union emblem was retained for
a year or so, but, as the Puritans of New England had misgiv-
ings about the cross it incorporated for religious reasons, it
was resolved in 1777 to drop it and substitute a blue field with
13 five-pointed white stars, one for each state in the union. It
was the first national flag in the world to include stars. What
inspired the Americans to choose stars is not clear. Perhaps
they were trying to say that they saw their young state as "a
new constellation in the firmament of nations." Perhaps
ancient ideas of the star as a symbol of hope, good fortune ("to
be born under a lucky star"), or immortality were a factor.

The American stars, however, were to become a new and
powerful symbol in themselves. They were seen all over the
world as symbols of freedom, republicanism, and independence of the Old World and its dynasties. The five-pointed
stars (and the stripes) were copied in a number of countries
that were inspired by America's example, first of all Chile in
seceding from Spain in 1817, then Liberia in 1847, Cuba in
1850, and several others. During the American civil war in 1864
a European commentator wrote that "the working men of
Europe felt instinctively that the star-spangled banner carried

the destiny of their class." The commentator's name? Karl Marx.

When the Russian communists overthrew the Tsarist regime in 1917 and replaced the eagle with a new form of national arms—a globe with a hammer and sickle surmounting a rising sun and at the top a five-pointed red star—it is possible that this very idea of a five-pointed star was derived from the American flag. To the early Communists, as to the Chileans in 1817, the United States was a model and a source of inspiration, and the American flag was the banner of liberty. The Stars and Stripes and the Red Star—one of many ironies in the history of symbols.

Colors

Red is the most popular of all colors. Ask a candy seller or a toy manufacturer. In Russian the word for "beautiful"—*krásivy*—comes from the same root as the word for "red"—*krásny.*

Naturally enough, the word "red" is also connected with the word for "blood." In Sanskrit "blood" is *rudhira*; in Old Norse, *rodra.* Through blood red is associated with life, emotion, passion, warmth, heat, fire, bloodshed, bravery ("the red badge of courage"), sacrifice, and danger. All this is reflected in language: "to see red," "to paint the town red," "to be caught red-handed."

In symbolism red stands first and foremost for "love" in every sense of the word: being and falling in love, making love, neighborly love, love of God, and God's love of man. What cannot be expressed in words can be said with a red rose: "Celestial rosy red, love's proper hue."

At the same time red is the color of war and battle. When the Vikings wanted to show that they came with warlike intentions, they displayed a red shield on their masts. It was a declaration of war. In the Danish navy a red flag was the signal to attack. Red is the military color: in Britain, Denmark, and other

Even without color this picture of flags waving in the wind suggests the symbolic power of red banners; on one hand invigorating and inspiring; on the other frightening and menacing. The picture shows Social Democrats demonstrating in Copenhagen in 1935. The hammer and scythe in the corner of the flag was the emblem of the Social Democratic youth movement.

countries army uniforms were red. Red is the color of Mars, the god of war,as it is of the planet Mars in alchemy.

Nowadays red is perhaps also the most predominant of all political symbols, signifying revolution, socialism, communism. Red Front. Red Army. Red Mother. The Red Dean. During the French Revolution the red bonnet of the Jacobins symbolized the most extreme republicanism. In 1860 Garibaldi contributed to the overthrow of the old royal houses of Italy with his famous Red Shirts.

The most characteristic manifestation of the red color of revolution, however, is the red flag. Its earliest known use was during a revolt of French silk workers at Lyons in 1834. In the following decades red flags turned up during strikes and demonstrations all over Europe. After the Communist victory in Russia in 1917 the red banner was adopted as the national flag of the Soviet Union. Since then communists everywhere have virtually adopted the red flag, so much so that the Social Democrats of West Germany have felt so uneasy at sharing the color with them that they have considered changing their party color to blue or orange.

Red probably registers more quickly than other colors, particularly in the dark and in fog. This fact is reflected in communications: in ambulances and fire engines, in danger signals and in the red "stop" sign at traffic lights.

In the Church red symbolizes Christ's passion as well as the fire of the Holy Ghost, and it is thus the color of Whitsun. In the Roman Catholic Church especially red also stands for the blood of the martyrs. Since 1245 it has been the distinctive color of cardinals. This last fact led Victor Hugo to call the lobster "the cardinal of the sea," to which a witty Norwegian retorted that it would have been an apt simile if cardinals first turned red in purgatory.

Blue

Heaven in most religions is the abode of the gods or at any rate of the chief of them. So it is little wonder that blue, celestially beautiful blue, should have become the color of the celestial gods. The Greek god Zeus was shown clad in blue, as were the Roman Jupiter and his wife Juno. The Scandinavian god Odin also seems to have worn blue. With the advance of Christianity the Virgin Mary was depicted in blue. Her blue robe and more especially her blue cloak, which gave shelter to the poor and persecuted, can be seen in thousands of representations, not least in the ones where she is shown as the Queen of Heaven: "clothed with the sun, and the moon under her feet," in the words of Revelation.

From the dress of Mary, blue passed to hundreds of coats of arms, among others those of ecclesiastical personages and institutions and of towns whose church was consecrated to her. Above all, however, blue became the color of the French coat of arms. As the emblem of France the French kings chose neither a lion nor an eagle but lilies, symbol of the purity of Mary, gold on blue, Mary's color. Along with purple blue became the color of royalty: the kings of France, the kings of England, the Swedish kings. The sash of high royal orders was usually blue; e.g. the British Order of the Garter, the Danish Order of the Elephant, the Swedish Order of the Seraphim, and the French Order of the Holy Ghost.

From these derive the terms "cordon bleu" and "blue ribbon," indicating distinction, excellence, or outstanding quality. In Denmark "blue stamp," originally used for branding prime-quality food, carries the same meaning, while the Danish *Who's Who?* is called "The Blue Book." In Spain the nobility

The word "heaven" was originally associated with "cloak." Mary, the Queen of Heaven, in her blue cloak became one of the most popular themes of Christian art, especially in the 13th and 14th centuries when figures and pictures of the cloaked Madonna became known as a protection against the plague. This picture is from a French woodcut dated 1524.

were said to have "blue blood," an expression that has spread to many other countries. From the gods blue passed to their adherents. Blue became the color of loyalists, standing for lawfulness. In Sweden and Britain it is the color of the Conservatives.

From the celestial gods blue also took quite a different direction. It stood in ancient times for divine wisdom. It was the color of truth, and in the Church it became the color of faith. Blue signifies fidelity (the blue forget-me-not), honesty, innocence, chastity. Blue eyes (at least in latitudes where they are usual) are considered to indicate a person without guile but can also metaphorically mean somebody whose integrity approaches the naive.

Besides the sky, of course, the sea is blue. But in symbolism it has not had much significance as such. Naval uniforms in almost every country are dark, or navy, blue, but whether this is at all symbolical is questionable.

On the other hand, there is much symbolism in blue as the color of distance. Before the First World War French military uniforms were "horizon blue," the camouflage of those days. The term "the blue mountains" suggests nostalgia, wanderlust, and romanticism—the "blue blossom of Poetry," "into the blue." Blue is associated with sadness, *Weltschmerz*, melancholy, "the blue hour," *Mood Indigo*, the blues.

The blueness of the air may also come into this category. Light blue is popular for air-force uniforms and with air services. And, as everybody knows, it is blue for a little boy, pink for a girl. When a Frenchman's wife gives birth to a baby boy, he will put a blue cornflower, a *bleuet*, in his buttonhole.

Yellow

The dual and contradictory symbolism of yellow is connected with the fact that both the sun and gall are that color. Strangely enough, the latter seems to have made the greater impact.

The ancient Greeks believed that a person's humor, character, and personality depended on body fluids. Important among these was gall. An excess of gall was the principal reason why people became choleric (the word means "having too much gall"). This in turn led to a number of other adverse characteristics, it was thought. This theory of "the temperaments" was a significant factor in the Middle Ages.

The yellowness of gall came to symbolize envy and jealousy, spite, malice, guile, deceit, heresy, faithlessness, treachery, and several other forms of infamy or wickedness. Yellow be-

The Latin phrase *Fovet et ornat* in a printer's mark dates from the beginning of the 17th century and means "it warms and lights" or, more poetically, "it caresses and beautifies." The reference, of course, is to the sun, but it could apply equally to yellow, which took over much of the sun's symbolism.

came a mark of disgrace, the badge of ignominy. Imposters, perjurers, and false witnesses were condemned to wear yellow hats. In art Judas, the archtraitor, was portrayed wearing a yellow cloak; Synagoga, the personification of Jewry, likewise. In 1215 the Church decreed that Jews should wear a yellow badge. Some seven centuries later Hitler did the same. Yellow was the color of prostitution and more recently would seem to have carried a veiled allusion to homosexuality. In English-speaking countries "yellow" is synonymous with cowardice.

Yet none of this can conceal the fact that the sun and gold are yellow (the two words have the same root). Yellow stood for the king of metals, for wealth and splendor, as well as for the light of the world, for glory and sanctity. In classical times yellow was the color of the sun god Apollo, and today (with white) it is the Pope's color. Yellow stands for divinity and royalty and, from these, generosity, magnanimity, nobility, and wisdom.

So it was with the white race, and it is little wonder that yellow enjoyed at least as much respect with yellow people. In China yellow was the most distinguished of all colors, in certain periods reserved to the emperor. He alone was allowed to wear the color.

Green

The word "green" comes from the same root as "grow," and it originally meant no more than "growing." Similarly, green stands for what grows, for the living as opposed to the dead or lifeless; for vegetation, growth, fertility, vitality, life itself.

In the desert especially green denotes the difference between life and death, and perhaps for that reason it became the special color of the Prophet Mohammed. Through his son-in-law, Ali, it passed to the caliphs, and today it is one of the sacred colors of Islam, present in the flags of nearly every Muslim country.

Above all, of course, spring is green, as is youth ("the salad days"). Green symbolizes thaw, rebirth, and regeneration, the renewal of life and of all things. To the religious reformers of the 16th century it was the color of Protestantism, signifying God's "renewed Church" as opposed to the effete and sterile

The evergreen leaves of hope are combined with another symbol of hope, the anchor, in this 17th-century English printer's mark. *Floreat in aeternum* ("Flourish for ever") may have been the printer's own expressed wish.

Church of Rome.

Where there is life, there is hope, and perhaps more than anything else green is the color of hope. It was so in antiquity, and it is so today. This aspect of the symbolism of green is particularly associated with evergreens, plants that retain their greenness when the rest of nature is withered and leafless, bare, somber, and dead. If such plants can remain green through the winter, then surely man can survive death and attain to everlasting life. To the Greeks and the Romans the cypress, the myrtle, the ivy, and the laurel, among other plants, suggested such ideas; to Gauls and Scandinavians, the mistletoe; to Germans, the fir tree; today the Christmas tree that we bring indoors to sustain our hope during the depth of winter.

In the Church, too, green stood for hope, which was one of the three cardinal virtues of Christianity (with faith and charity), fortified in this case, perhaps, by the reflected green of the Garden of Eden. In art a green cloak characterizes St. Anne, the mother of Mary who gave birth to "the Hope of the World." Was it as an extension of this symbolism of hope that green was chosen as the color of the Council of Europe and the European Movement? Road signs in the European network are green.

The fact that green was the color of spring, renewal, and hope made it also that of freedom. The ancient custom of the May tree gave rise in the 18th century to the "liberty tree." The green tree came to symbolize popular liberty, bearing fresh foliage after the winter of tyranny. In North America liberty trees played a significant role in the War of Independence. The first was set up in Boston in 1765. The idea spread, and, when war broke out in 1775, the colonists advanced to the attack under banners with a green tree. It was not until a year or so later that this flag was superseded by the Stars and Stripes. Perhaps the greatest period of the liberty tree was after 1789; to the French Revolution the green tree was a fanfare proclaiming the right of every man to be free. When the new ideas reached Italy and a revolutionary flag had to be found, the French flag was taken as a model. The Italians chose a tricolor but with a difference: the blue stripe was replaced with a green one, symbolizing freedom and a republican constitution. It was the first national flag in the world to contain green.

Is it fortuitous that traffic lights turn green to indicate the opposite of "stop?" At least it is not an unbridgeable gulf between life, hope, and liberty on the one hand and "the green light" on the other.

Green, evergreen, continuing life,
procreation—you may kiss any girl or boy under
the evergreen mistletoe.

Black

"And God saw the light, that it was good: and God divided the light from the darkness." Yes, the light is good. It is beautiful, appealing, warming, comforting, and reassuring. Darkness and blackness are the opposite of all these.

Underlying this feeling, of course, is a physical and psychological influence (which is no doubt true of all symbolism of color). How and why can be hard to say, but that does not make it any the less real.

Black stood for night, fear, misfortune, annihilation, death. The grave in the black earth was the first stage on the way to the Underworld, which was as black as Paradise, or Elysium, was gleaming white. The gods that were associated with the realm of death all had black as their distinguishing color: Hecate, Ceres, and Pluto on his ebony throne. The Christian Hell was also black, and there the Prince of Darkness reigned. When seen on earth, at a Black Mass, for example, he was invariably accompanied by a black dog or a black cat. And the very sight of a black cat could be a bad omen. In Church art the traitor Judas Iscariot is sometimes portrayed with a black halo.

With death and burial came grief, and black above all was the color of mourning, for which we have documentary evidence as far back as the death of Alexander the Great in 323 B.C. Widows and other mourners wore black. Mourning notepaper was black-edged, as were mourning stamps. Anarchist flags are black (dating probably from 1871), because, as some people think, anarchism desires the death and burial of all government and authority. Or is the anarchist flag rather another version of the black pirate flag, to be regarded as a threat of "your money or your life," the abolition of the right to property?

Stamps with his portrait edged in black were issued when President Paul von Hindenburg of Germany died in 1934. Black mourning stamps have also been issued on other occasions.

The ancient Greeks believed that there was a connection between man's black gall and his disposition to melancholy. At any rate they associated black with despondency, gloom, and melancholy—Dr. Johnson's "black dog." Above all black came to be the color of the Church, the Protestant no less than the Catholic. In dress and in church furniture it was used as a conscious expression of devotion, awareness of sin, repentance, penance, self-denial, contempt for "this world." Bibles and hymn books are invariably black, looking, it has been said, as if they had been bound by malignant hands. By wearing black one demonstrated one's piety, gravity, and chastity, one's rejection of vanity: a tendency that was only intensified by religious and political upheavals—the triumph of Puritanism in the 17th century, the French revolutions of 1789, 1830, 1848, and 1871, even the Russian revolution of 1917. Black stood for middle-class respectability, whatever the name given to this reality.

Much of this symbolism is reflected in language: "black" occurs in a great many expressions of shame, despair, lawlessness, reaction, obscurity, and other blameworthy activities: "a black look," "a black lookout," "a black mark," "a black mood," "blackball," "in one's black books," "blackmail," "blackguard," "black-letter day," "black money." The "black sheep" of the family was "blacklisted" for trading on "the black market."

This symbolism, of course, is as the white man sees it. To him white is beautiful and praiseworthy and black the opposite. Many blacks have inherited the white man's language and with it thousands of built-in attitudes. Against at least one of these attitudes, however, the blacks have understandably begun to protest, and their protest is "Black is beautiful."

Quite different is the cult of black by Fascism and Nazism. When Mussolini started his Fascist movement in 1919, he dressed his supporters in black shirts, and they soon came to be known simply as "the Blackshirts". The choice of color is said to have been inspired by the black dress of the Italian rural working class and by the fact that black is practical in a hot climate. But how much lay in the fact that black is a frightening and menacing color, expressing insensitivity and brutality?

The Nazi color was at first brown, but this was eventually

changed, and, especially after Hitler's accession to power in 1933, black became the preferred color. The SS wore black; the Hitler Jugend wore black, as did several other central organs of Nazism. This was undoubtedly connected with a historical German inclination. It has been shown that in medieval heraldry black was twice or three times as common in Germany as in other countries. The cross of the order of Teutonic Knights was black, its dress black and white, and the arms of the Hohenzollern dynasty black and white. The colors of Prussia came to be black and white; hundreds of public and private coats of arms were black and white; cockades, boundary posts, insignias, uniforms were black and white; all official ornamentations were black and white; the Iron Cross was black; and black (an·otherwise extremely rare color in flags) appears in the flags of the Weimar Republic, Bismarck's Germany, and both East and West Germany.

In some degree the Nazi cult of black was an extension of this historical tendency. But to a wide extent it also exploited the hostile, malevolent, and brutal feelings and sentiments that black can express or suggest. This was made abundantly clear in the black SS uniform with the death's head in the cap. It looked like a death sentence and was meant to. The Nazi black was intended to express both human contempt and fearlessness of death.

But if the use of black by the Nazis can be thus explained, there are one or two other questions one cannot help asking.

Today the pirate flag is either a joke or a plaything. Whether it was ever used in real life is doubtful, but that does not affect its symbolism. There can be no doubt as to the meaning of the black.

Why was black already so common in medieval German heraldry? And why did the Germans retain their liking for this color for centuries? Did the universality and official status of black, especially in Prussia, help to influence German mentality and national character in a "black" direction?

White

A thing can be dark red or pale blue, but it cannot be more or less white. There are no shades of white. White is something absolute. Regardless of what "white" may be to the scientist or optician, by everyone else it is regarded as something absolutely "pure" and unmixed. And that is what it stands for symbolically: for purity in every sense of the term.

The pure and unsullied is also the holy. "Put off thy shoes!" The priests of ancient temples were generally clad in white, as were the Celtic druids. Several of the Catholic Church's orders of monks and nuns wear white, and white is supreme in the Church's hierarchy of color. It is the color of the Pope, who always wears white.

Sacrificial animals—doves, oxen, lambs—were preferably white, without a speck of any other color. The Roman historian Tacitus tells us that the Germans worshipped white horses, which they kept in sacred groves. And when King Christian X of Denmark crossed the border into North Schleswig, which had voted to return to Denmark in a plebiscite, in 1920, no efforts were spared to find him a horse that was milk white from ears to tail.

In the New Testament white is mentioned again and again as a term for divinity, glory, and "transfiguration." St. Matthew says, for example, of Jesus (17:2): "He was transfigured before them: and his face did shine as the sun, and his raiment was white as the light." Revelation tells of a "great multitude," of the chosen, the righteous, the redeemed, "clothed with white robes." White is the color of grace, as it is of faith. The walls of Protestant, especially Reformed, churches are white. Christening robes are white, because baptism cleanses away sin.

To be "pure" is also to be "untouched." White expresses innocence, chastity, and virginity. The Roman vestals wore white as a sign of their chaste habits. For the same reason

It could not be whiter. These Roman Catholic girls on the way to their first Communion are dressed all in white—white dresses and blouses, white shoes, white stockings and gloves. They are wearing a white wreath and carry a white handbag, a hymnbook bound in white, and a large white candle. This is an impressive symbolical manifestation of purity, innocence, virginity, and youth.

brides wear (or wore) white, as do girls when they are confirmed. The primary attribute of the virgin Mary is the white lily, symbolic of her immaculate conception.

Akin to white as the color of innocence is its role as a symbol of friendship and peace. When the Vikings approached a coast on an errand of peace, they mounted a white shield on their masts. Negotiators between warring tribes have from ancient times carried a peeled white staff to show that they came without hostile intent. Later a white armband or a white flag was used, and these can also indicate a truce, surrender, capitulation. Perhaps there is a connection with the white feather that in Britain symbolized cowardice.

The white flag of the Red Cross might seem to be connected with white as a signal for the end of hostilities. The likeness, however, is fortuitous: the flag of the Red Cross was created by Henri Dunant, a Swiss, as the reverse of the colors of the Swiss flag. The white of Red Cross ambulances and hospital buildings may also derive from the general antiseptic white of the medical profession, which, like that of the food trade, serves the practical purpose of revealing dirt more readily than a darker background would. Whiteness here is intended to promote sterility, as it undoubtedly does, in more senses than one. There can be something cold and arid in all this white, inducing feelings of loneliness and despair.

Can there be a link between the coldness of white (connected with the whiteness of sanctity) and white as a color of mourning? Along with black (and to some extent purple) it used to be the color of death, of funerals and mourning. The custom is known from antiquity—in China, for example. In some countries even today coffins have to be white, and most people would probably consider white flowers to be most appropriate at a funeral. This may have some connection with the fact that white is also the color of resurrection.

White symbolizes a pure life, a lofty moral code, and divine mercy: it was perhaps as a reflection of this that the kings of France took white for their color. It can be traced back to the 15th century. But white became particularly famous as the royal color of France under the Bourbons, dating from 1589. The national flag of France up to the Revolution in 1789 was white with three golden lilies. In that year, however, the National Guard combined the white of the royal house with the red and blue of the arms of Paris to form a red-white-and-blue cockade, the basis of the future Tricolor. On royal commemorative days French royalists and "legitimists" still wear a white carnation.

To return to purity: the Latin word *candidus* means both "white" and "honest" (candid). A Roman who was nominated for public office would always wear a white toga during the election campaign in order to demonstrate his integrity and probity. It was termed a *toga candida*, and the man himself was called *candidatus*, from which we get the word "candidate." The white stood for honesty, veracity, loyalty, qualities that cannot be adulterated or at any rate should not. From these in turn we get truth, wisdom, bliss, joy, and goodness. The fact that this last category of ideas can also be denoted by whiteness may also, however, be connected with a different symbolism altogether, namely that which derives from milk——mother's milk and the milk we get from ruminants—man's most basic food. "The milk of human kindness," as Shakespear says in *Macbeth.*

Another domain in which only the pure and unadulterated will serve is honor. White stood for honor, male and female, the knight's and the maiden's. The whiteness of honor was often illustrated by an ermine in its winter coat. It was believed that the ermine would die of shame if it got the slightest of stains on its white fur. A spotless character, an unblemished reputation, a life without fear or reproach, was what the white ermine stood for. It was often accompanied by the Latin motto *Potius mori quam foederi* ("Rather die than be tarnished"). The swan can also represent whiteness (see "The Swan").

It should perhaps be mentioned that white, like black, has a role (at any rate in the symbolism of language) as what one might call an "antipathetic" color. White is optically antipathetic to black and, perhaps mainly through body color, to red. If communists and revolutionaries are "red," their opponents are "white." In 1917 there were said to be "white" armies and "white" generals in Russia and Finland. And if a lie is normally "black," there is also a "white" lie. It is a pardonable and perhaps even a praiseworthy one. And so *white.*

The Vegetable Kingdom

The Oak

A lady telephoned for advice. She was attending an anniversary celebration and wished on behalf of a group of friends to present some oak cuttings to a gardener while making a short speech. Oak trees were supposed to symbolize something, were they not?

They do indeed. What the lion is among quadrupeds and the eagle among birds the oak is among trees. The oak's strength and longevity, together with its beauty and grandeur when fully grown, made it sacred to the highest of the ancient Greek gods, Zeus. This may also have been because tall oaks, which towered above other trees, were thought to attract lightning to a particular degree, and Zeus was also the god of thunder. Oak was the best of all known woods. Hercules' club was of oak. The oak became the symbol of sublimity, strength, and long life. These are qualities which inspire awe, trust and confidence, and so the picture of an oak tree is often used today by institutions wishing to be regarded with such feelings, such as banks and insurance companies.

The oak generally stands for the ideals of active, patriotic, local citizens, from which it is a short step to the political ideals of self-rule and democracy. Acorns, oak leaves, or oak trees are therefore common in municipal heraldry. The picture shows a British municipal coat of arms.

To the Romans the oak was the tree of Jupiter, and they honored it perhaps even more highly than the Greeks did. The Latin word *robur* means not only oak and oak wood but also vitality and physical and moral strength ("robustness"), the "flower" of the army and the country's youth, "heart of oak." The highest honor a Roman soldier could attain, by risking his life to save a comrade's, was the "oak wreath" or "oak crown." When anyone wearing this decoration of oak leaves around his head appeared in an auditorium, perhaps the amphitheater, the audience would rise. The wreath of oak leaves stood for self-sacrificing comradeship, bravery, and patriotism, and this symbolism has carried over into modern times. Oak wreaths, leaves, or acorns occur in numerous military decorations, among them the German Iron Cross "with oak leaves," insignias, badges of rank, and other national or military ornamentation.

To the Celts of Gaul and Britain the oak was a sacred tree. Trials took place under an oak tree. Offerings and human sacrifices were hung from special oaks. Large and old oaks have been objects of veneration and superstition all over Europe. Oak trees, branches, and leaves occur in the arms of numerous European families, as, for example, the Italian princely family della Rovere ("of the oak") and the Prussian noble family of Bismarck (three oak leaves). The oak is the state tree of six American states: Connecticut, Georgia, Illinois, Iowa, Maryland, and New Jersey and of Washington, D.C.

The acorn also occurs frequently in ornamentation and heraldry, unconsciously or perhaps consciously with sexual overtones. In anatomical terminology the tip of the penis is called the "glans," or acorn.

To recapitulate: the oak is dedicated to Zeus and the Roman Jupiter. It originally symbolized two things: strength, solidity, constancy ("the right stuff"), and longevity; and tenacity, bravery, magnanimity, comradeship until death, and other soldierly virtues. In time, however, the oak has also come to

The oak enters into the national symbolism of nearly every country in Europe but perhaps nowhere more so than in Germany, where it is the very essence of Germanism. When Friedrich Wilhelm III of Prussia instituted the Iron Cross for bravery as part of the struggle to liberate Germany from the French in 1813, he placed oak leaves in the center of the cross.

represent the ideals that characterize the independent, self-supporting, free man. It stands for public spirit, political service, self-rule, patriotism, the "native land." Oaks, acorns, or oak leaves often appear in municipal heraldry and on coins. What one would read into the oak leaves here is partly up to oneself. Compatriotism, historical fellowship, national and democratic solidarity?

A huge oak tree is used in the United States and other countries to symbolize savings banks. Partly this is because of the oak's strength, toughness, and longevity and partly, no doubt, because the mighty tree started as a small acorn. It is the sort of symbolism anybody can understand.

The Fleur-de-lis

Everyone knows the beautiful trisected device that is called the fleur-de-lis, or flower-de-luce. It is a very old device, occurring as an ornament or symbol in Mesopotamian and Egyptian art a thousand years or more before the birth of Christ.

That it is meant to represent a flower, or plant, can scarcely be in doubt, but whether it is a lily is less certain. Perhaps originally the device was a highly simplified representation of a date palm, to people of the desert a sacred tree signifying the difference between life and death: water, food, and shade. As a symbol the device stood for life, growth, sanctity. *also a stylized male genitals*

The device appears to have arrived in western Europe in the Middle Ages and to have been regarded as a lily or iris. The iris, especially the white one, had stood since antiquity for purity, innocence and virginity and had been the most popular symbol of the Virgin Mary. The stylized iris soon passed into Marian symbolism. The relative ease with which it could be drawn probably contributed to its popularity, and the beautiful

The French royal arms, including the *fleur de lis*, golden on a blue field, in a version dating from the end of the 15th century. Originally the arms of French kings were "strewn" or patterned with an indefinite number of lilies. But by about 1365 the number had become fixed at three, corresponding to the Trinity. The lilies themselves were regarded as symbols of the Virgin Mary.

device spread all over Europe. It is found in thousands of coats of arms, including the arms of towns and cities whose churches were consecrated to the Virgin.

The device achieved its greatest fame as a heraldic emblem, however, because the kings of France incorporated it in their arms. For centuries the "fleur-de-lis," three stylized golden irises in a blue field, constituted the most celebrated arms in Europe. When the monarchy came to an end during the French Revolution, the fleur-de-lis was also abolished. To display it was a punishable offense. It was pulled down from palaces and public buildings, sawn out of wrought-iron gates, cut from the bindings of books. It is seen hardly anywhere in France today.

Outside France the fleur-de-lis lived on, however. For centuries it had represented not only the French kings and the French state but had also stood for everything that was regarded as specifically French, including France as the European center of ladies' fashions. The fleur-de-lis was associated with French taste and French elegance, with *haute couture,* and with other ways that women have of making themselves attractive. All over the world the fleur-de-lis was adopted as the emblem of fashion houses, perfumeries, and beauty parlors. It graced the wrappings of toilet soap, silk stockings, and coquettish underwear.

But it also stood for something quite different. When the British officer Robert Baden-Powell founded the Scout movement in 1908, he chose for its badge a similar device, not from the French emblem but the device that is used in the compass. The part of a compass dial that points north is often designed by a fleur-de-lis. To Baden-Powell the compass needle's northward-pointing "fleur-de-lis" symbolized "true course." It denoted the ideals of the Scout movement as a fixed point in life, a never-failing guideline that always pointed to the Pole Star, the only celestial body that never moves but stays unwavering at its post in the firmament. And so today the fleur-de-lis is chiefly noted for two things: it is the lily of ladies and of Boy Scouts.

The Daisy

Most people like flowers, and many have a favorite flower that appeals to them more than any other either because of its color, its form, its scent, or its associations with childhood or some happy memory. In this respect rulers do not differ from other people, and just because they have been rulers, their favorite flowers have sometimes gone down in history.

In the 12th century there was a French count, Geoffrey of Anjou, who was so fond of the broom (*planta genista*), which flourished all over his domains, that he always wore a sprig of it in his cap. He was therefore called in French, Geoffroi Plante-Genet; and, when his son ascended the English throne in 1154 as Henry II, the dynasty came to be known as the House of Plantagenet. Later on the rose became the special favorite of English royalty. In the 15th century a red rose was the official badge of the collateral line that called itself the House of Lancaster, while a white rose stood for the House of York. The long and bloody struggle between these two royal lines, lasting from 1455 to 1485, is known as the Wars of the Roses.

Female rulers called Margaret (Marguerite, Margareta, Margrethe) have often chosen the daisy, or marguerite, whose name they have shared, as their special flower, although in

Princess Margrethe of Denmark—from 1972 Queen Margrethe—was born in April 1940, and soon after the court jeweler put on the market a "Margrethe" (marguerite) pin, which quickly became extremely popular. This was connected with the fact that during the German occupation of Denmark (1940–1945) it was regarded as an expression of loyalty to the Danish royal family and also a (modest) manifestation of patriotism. It is still one of the most characteristic adornments of Danish women.

popular speech it may have gone under different names. (The flower's English name means "day's eye.") In the symbolism of flowers the daisy, according to some sources, stands for innocence, according to others for love (which, of course, need not be mutually exclusive), and more than any other flower it is used as the oracle of love. "He loves me! He loves me not! He loves me!"

One of the royal ladies who had the daisy as her flower was Princess Margaret of Great Britain (1882–1920), a grandchild of Queen Victoria who married the late King Gustavus VI of Sweden. When their daughter Ingrid married the then Crown Prince Frederik of Denmark in 1935, her father gave her a piece of jewelry in the design of a daisy as a memento of her mother. In 1967 when Margrethe, the daughter of Frederik and Ingrid, was married, she wore her mother's daisy on her wedding dress. Her bridal bouquet included the large oxeye daisy, the commonest and cheapest flower in Denmark but one of the most beautiful and her own. And what did the bridegroom, Prince Henrik, hold in his hand when he waved to the crowd? A rose? A carnation? No, an oxeye daisy—a marguerite!

The Wreath

In the early 1950s the Egyptian archaeologist Zakaria Goneim was engaged in excavating the pyramid of King Sekemket at Saqqara in northern Egypt. Sekemket reigned in about the year 2600 B.C. When Goneim arrived at the actual burial chamber, he found it intact. As far as could be judged, nobody— priest, grave robber or archaeologist—had set foot there since the chamber had been sealed over 4,500 years before. In the chamber stood the king's tomb, carved from a single huge block of alabaster, and on the lid lay a wreath.

Similar wreaths have been found in other Egyptian graves, and the Egyptian *Book of the Dead* explains their purpose. The wreath was a reward for a successful judgment on a man's works at the end of his life, and a promise of everlasting life. The wreath, the ring, and the circle are common symbols of eternity.

Notwithstanding the fact that this explanation of the wreath is some thousands of years old, it is scarcely the right one and at any rate not the primary one. The essence of the wreath on the coffin is not its form but its material. Apart from the royal mummy itself, the wreath was the only organic matter in this burial chamber. The sprigs, the flowers, the foliage that made up the wreath were the dead king's link with life and life's forces. The Egyptian word *ankh* means both "wreath" and "life." When conversation turns on a subject that arouses forebodings or if one of the company feels uneasy, he will knock on wood or say "Touch wood." The original point of this action was to touch the tree. From time immemorial men have believed that to touch a plant or a tree gave protection against evil forces. The vital forces of the living and growing thing constituted a safeguard and also involved cleansing, physical as well as moral. The vegetative force took away the guilt from any misdeeds one might have committed. To touch plants meant "remission of sins" (millennia before Christianity coined the phrase). This is probably what underlies the original use of the wreath. The effect was presumably the same, whatever the flora employed—branches, sprays, bouquets— but a wreath was both beautiful and practical. You could wear it on your head, hang it around an animal's neck, decorate buildings with it. The wreath came to be the commonest form of the "vital" parts of the plant.

In ancient Greece the wreath was used especially on occasions or in ceremonies of initiation, the start of something important, a dedication, an inauguration. The plants used would often be those associated with the gods involved. Each god had his specific plants. In some sacrifices it was not only those who sacrificed, the priests, and the statues of the gods that were wreathed. The animal and other offerings as well as the temple's altar, columns, and walls would be embellished with wreaths.

At weddings both the bride and groom and the guests were wreathed. The wreaths might be of quince leaves or marjoram, as the quince was sacred to Juno, the goddess of marriage, and marjoram was associated with Hymen, the wedding god. ("Hymen's chains" would doubtless be plaited from marjoram.) But they were usually of myrtle, the plant of Venus, the goddess of love. In ceremonial processions and at sacred and secular banquets the participants would decorate themselves

In the classical world the participants in a symposium might be wreathed, and the wreath became inseparable from wine merchants and innkeepers. The picture shows a Scandinavian inn with a wreath as a sign. Woodcut from a history of the Scandinavian people by Olaus Magnus, 1555.

with vine leaves or ivy branches. Both plants belonged to Bacchus, the god of wine. An ivy wreath was also the sign of wine sellers, and into modern times a green wreath (of whatever plant) has served as a tavern sign. At funerals the family and other mourners attending the funeral feast wore wreaths of the evergreen cypress, which was dedicated to Pluto, the god of the Underworld. The dead person was also wreathed, and the coffin would be decorated with wreaths. In the Roman Empire the wreath became a common motif on tombs and gravestones.

The wreath also had its function at ceremonies in commemoration of a dead person, and from this we come to another sphere where it played a big part: as a prize for the winner of a sports contest (and later for a victor in war). To win the "wreath" became synonymous with being victorious. The athletic games which meant so much to the social life of ancient Greece appear to have originated as memorial festivals for dead "heroes." The winner of an athletic event was awarded a wreath in memory of this hero, and the wreath was usually hung up afterward in the temple of the god who was the games' patron or who had helped to ensure victory.

At the Isthmian Games in Corinth, which were dedicated to Pan, the victory wreaths were of parsley or pine leaves, and at the Nemean Games they were of wild celery. The Olympic Games, the most celebrated of all (the year of their foundation, 776 B.C., was the starting point of the Greek calendar), were under the patronage of Zeus himself, and the victory wreath was of wild olives, which (together with the oak) were sacred to Zeus and his daughter, Pallas Athene. Even more important in the history of the wreath were the Pythian Games at Delphi. They were dedicated to Apollo, and the winners were crowned with wreaths of sprigs from the sacred tree of Apollo, the laurel. Not only physical sports were involved: the events also included music, poetry, and declamation, and the laurel wreath that was awarded to the victors in these artistic contests was to become one of the most familiar and lasting of the white man's symbols. The laurel wreath became an image of poetry and poetic talents. Great poets (and also in time lesser ones) were called *laureatus* ("laureled"). Laurel wreaths were incorporated in poets' coats of arms, among them that of the German poet Friedrich Schiller. The laurel wreath could also symbolize other arts and intellectual achievements in a wider sense, for example in philosophy and science. The evergreen wreath became an image of the immortal name that might be won through intellectual creativity.

The Romans extended the laurel's scope. Laurels could now be awarded for military achievement, patriotic service in war, heroism, and generalship. Generals who were given a "triumph," a martial parade through Rome at the head of victorious legions, were crowned with a laurel wreath. In time laurels came to stand for illustrious achievements in almost any sphere of life. And it was said of one who conserved his energy when the wreath of honor had been won that he "was resting on his laurels." Other Roman distinctions were the grass wreath, the fennel wreath (for victorious gladiators), and the famous oak wreath that was awarded to soldiers who had saved a comrade's life on the battlefield by risking their own. Later the oak wreath also came to represent other forms of patriotic service, for example political activity.

The Greeks had previously awarded a wreath as a mark of homage or distinction to civic personages and distinguished

Bellona, goddess of war, surrounded by her implements: lances, halberds, armor, helmets, shields, swords, drums, bows and arrows, and cannon. She is holding in one hand the palm of victory, while with the other she exhibits the triumphal wreath. German printer's mark, 1579.

foreigners, including heads of state. And almost inevitably the protecting, initiating, cleansing, and rewarding wreath, the wreath of victory, honor, and triumph, gradually became an almost permanent head decoration of rulers, kings, and eventually the Roman emperors. The ruler's wreath expressed sublimity, divinity, and sovereignty. Its leaves and fruit were soon made in gold and precious stones, and, together with another emblem of the ruler, the diadem, the jeweled circlet worn round the head, the wreath of gold gradually developed into what we call a "crown." To the Romans, indeed, it was roughly the same thing, as the Latin word *corona* means both "wreath" and "crown." An example illustrating the ancient conception of the wreath as an indication of royalty is the way in which the Roman soldiers mocked Jesus, putting a reed in his hand and a crown of thorns on his head and crying "Hail, King of the Jews!"

In the Old Testament of the Israelites wreaths and crowning with wreaths are mentioned on a number of occasions as expressions of joy, solemnity, or honor. The New Testament uses similar metaphors. For example, St. Paul speaks three or four times of "our crown of honor," "crown of righteousness," "incorruptible crown." Later the Church tried to eliminate wreaths and crowns from Christian life and language, and in the 3rd century several of the Fathers declaimed against them. But when the campaign proved to be in vain, as happened in so many other cases, what the Church could not extirpate it took over: the crown or wreath became a Christian symbol. It became God's reward to those who had "prevailed over death," chiefly the martyrs. In the mural paintings of the catacombs the hand of God can be seen stretching out from Heaven with a crown of victory. The wreath or crown also became an attribute of the great saints, including the apostles. And the bridal or virgin wreath became the mark of female saints and later of nuns, all of whom were "brides of Christ." On tombs and gravestones the wreath symbolized the resurrection and ever-

As a military, patriotic, and divinity symbol the wreath appealed strongly to Napoleon, and *two* wreaths were incorporated in the badge of the Legion of Honor that he founded in 1802, each consisting of half oak leaves and half laurels.

lasting life, "the unfading wreath of eternal life." Wreaths framed Christ's monogram and other sacred images and in time became merely a pious ornament or an ornament pure and simple.

In the Middle Ages the Christian use of the wreath to a large extent died away, but it enjoyed a new revival during the Renaissance and succeeding centuries. As a mark of distinction in intellectual life, the arts, military and state affairs, and sport it was almost supreme. Medals and decorations containing a wreath can be counted by the hundreds. The British institution of the poet laureate, whose duty was to compose odes on state occasions, arose from the custom in universities of presenting a laurel wreath to graduates in rhetoric and poetry. The winners of international bicycle races ride a *tour de triomphe* with a gigantic wreath around their head and one arm.

Rulers and leading intellectuals were portrayed crowned with a wreath, and when Napoleon had himself crowned in 1804, he actually wore a laurel wreath (of gold). Olive branches were from ancient times a sign of peace, and in classical antiquity a wreath of olives could mean peace. It still can. The emblem of the United Nations is a globe enclosed in a wreath of olives. In a church a wreath can mean the peace of God, and as a funeral and memorial symbol the wreath is more often employed than ever.

Artistic or religious immortality, heavenly or earthly reward, honor, distinction, fame, exalted rank, sovereignty, triumph, victory, peace, salvation, beatitude, happiness, festival, homage: Thorvaldsen, the famous sculptor, who used to crown himself and his guests before they sat at the table; the wife who lights the candles of the advent wreath four weeks before the "advent" of the Lord; the builders who hang up wreaths on completed buildings for the "topping-out" ceremony; and, the beginning of it all and still with us: the pleasure and the vitality associated with a wreath of fresh plants, woodruff, violets, or cowslips; the perfume of the flowers, the coolness of the leaves, the balm of touching green and growing things.

The Animal Kingdom

One of the most abusive epithets that can be applied to a person is to call him a pig or a swine. At the same time the diminutives, "piggy," "piggy-wiggy," are almost terms of endearment. As in speech so also in symbolism. "Pig," "swine," or "hog" stands for "repulsive," or "contemptible" yet at other times can denote something appealing, likable, or lucky.

To Jews and Muslims the pig is physically, religiously, and morally an abominable creature. "It is unclean unto you," says the law as set out in Deuteronomy, and the precept is taken seriously. Greeks and Romans took a different view. To them the pig symbolized the fertility and richness of nature, both nature in the wild and cultivated nature. With them it was the attendant (and votive offering) of a number of deities: Cybele, the earth goddess; Diana, goddess of the forest and of the chase; and Ceres, goddess of agriculture. To the Romans the wild pig or boar was also the symbol of something quite different. The wild boar is not a beast of prey: it does no harm to other animals. But it is fearless and defends itself at once if it

58

In pictures how is it possible to tell one saint from another? One can do so by means of their "attribute," something that characterizes them and by which they can be recognized, such as the keys of St. Peter and the tower of St. Barbara. A pig and a small bell are the attributes of St. Anthony, and it is chiefly by means of these that we can identify him. A T-shaped cross and a burning hand are also distinguishing marks of Anthony, and in this old woodcut (1494) we have them all.

feels threatened, even against much bigger creatures. To the Romans, therefore, the wild boar came to symbolize strength of character, self-confidence, and fearlessness, and they used figures of wild boars as military standards.

Few can have been fonder of the pig than the ancient Scandinavians. In Norse mythology a pig called Goldbrush was the mount of Freya, who was the goddess of rain, sunshine, crops, good harvest, and riches. Every day the gods in Valhalla ate roast pork from the hog Særimner. No matter how many were present, there was always plenty of meat, and the next day Særimner was whole again and could be slaughtered afresh. Perhaps it is an extension of this idea of the pig as the creature of fertility, affluence, and repletion that a savings bank often takes the form of a pig and is called a "piggy bank."

Christianity on the whole followed the Bible, and throughout the Middle Ages the pig symbolized all forms of filth (*Schweinerei*) and base instincts: unchastity, fornication, covetousness, greed, gluttony, intemperance, selfishness, anger, bad temper. Biblical descriptions of the wild boar as a destroyer of fields and vineyards contributed to this last image. The pig could stand for the designs and temptations of the Devil, even for the Antichrist himself.

As an image of demons overcome and temptations resisted the pig is the attribute of several saints, above all the popular hermit St. Anthony, who lived in Roman times in Egypt. Here the everyday life of the Middle Ages came into the picture. The Anthonites, the order of mendicant monks who took their name from Anthony, lived by keeping pigs. They were privileged to allow their pigs to find food wherever they wanted, and, in order that people might know they were Anthonite pigs that were rooting in their middens and not the unprivileged hogs of their neighbors, they had to wear a bell around their necks. It is by these—a pig or a bell or both—that St. Anthony can be recognized in art.

Horns

"Arise and thresh, O daughter of Zion: for I will make thine horn iron, and I will make thy hoofs brass: and thou shalt beat in pieces many people . . ." The skinny, tremulous man called the words into the empty chasm, and the echo came back from the mountainsides. It was in the scorching, salt-sparkling regions of the Dead Sea, and the man's name was Micah. The prophet Micah. God would intervene and punish the godless and would overthrow kings. The power of God was mightier than that of the others. God had horns.

Literally as far back as man can be traced, he has plainly regarded horned creatures with particular emotion. The cave paintings tell us how intensely the first hunters felt for aurochs, bison, deer, and reindeer; how ardently they wanted them and wanted to be like them. Later visual art and literature, not least the Bible, tell us of the nomad's and the farmer's fervent feelings for his oxen, goats, and sheep, of his admiration and love, indeed idolization and worship of them, and of how, like the hunter, he simply identified himself with them.

And it was in the horns that the cattle's soul and strength were concentrated. It was with their horns that the mighty oxen and rams butted, tossed, slung, *rammed*, gored, and killed. The Hebrew word *keren* means both "horn" and "power." If you were more than an ordinary man, if you were a superman or perhaps even a god, you had horns. Kings were portrayed bearing horns and had headdresses made with horns. The horns stood for strength, might, supremacy, sovereignty, royal dignity. They stood for sublimity and glory.

But horns were above all weapons, and it was chiefly in their capacity as killers that the kings bore horns. Horns were the sign of aggressiveness, overpowering ferocity, invincibility.

The caveman has dressed himself in an ox's hide with tail, head, and, above all, horns. Dancing for the rest of the tribe, he is no longer the man whom they thought they knew. He has horns on his head; he is more than a human being; he is on the way to becoming a god. Cave painting from the Dordogne, France.

Alexander the Great, after conquering Egypt, was declared divine in the temple of the ram god Amon. From then on he was usually shown on coins as wearing rams' horns, a sign of the ruler's divinity that was taken over by his successors, in this case Lysimakos of Thrace, on a coin from 306 B.C.

Warriors put horns on their helmets. This is known to have occurred from the earliest times: in Mesopotamia, by the Etruscans, in the Bronze Age in northern Europe, in the period of the Great Migrations, and not least in the age of chivalry. Every other aristocratic coat of arms in Scandinavia dating from the Middle Ages is furnished with horns, often with family names to match—Ox, Deer, Doe, Buck, Horn. The horns became almost a professional sign of the military class, with the connotation "militancy," "courage," "attack," "defense," "security," "victory," "deliverance," "honor," "dignity," "rank," and from these "pride" and "arrogance."

All this—strength, power, ferocity—was only one side of the symbolism of horns. The other was procreative vigor. The big males crushed their rivals, but with the females of the herd it was an altogether different side of their virility that they displayed. Here it was by reproducing numerous offspring that the bull manifested itself, and these powers were also exactly what his brother the king wanted. The male horns became a symbol of potency and fertility, of the ability—and desire—to copulate and beget children.

Perhaps the use of oxen for drawing the plow contributed to this symbolism. Plowing was an act of a sexual character, as anyone could see: the plow drew its furrow in the fertile soil. And it was to the ox's horns that the pulling ropes were fastened. The horns were the force behind the plow's coitus with the earth. Horns were an aphrodisiac and erotic stimulant. And not only *were*: to this day oriental chemists sell powdered rhinoceros (or unicorn!) horn to customers with declining virility. Could there be a connection here with the American word "horny?"

Whether there is a reverse connection between horns as a symbol of potency and as an attribute of cuckolds or deceived husbands, I cannot say. But certainly horns, and perhaps especially stags' horns, are an old symbol of cuckolds. "There will the Devil meet me, like an old cuckold, with horns on his head," says Beatrice in Shakespeare's *Much Ado about Nothing*. The archseducer in Wycherley's *The Country Wife* is significantly named Horner.

Progeny meant riches. A herd's forest of horns was the patriarch's most cherished sight, his assurance that God meant him well. Horns were a sign of good fortune, promise, fulfillment, and benediction. It is no accident that the metaphorical expression for abundance and prosperity in Greek mythology is a horn, what we call the "horn of plenty" (see a later chapter). The word "pecuniary," which means "of money," comes from the Latin *pecus*, meaning "cattle." The word "fee" has a similar derivation.

Physical strength and generative power—and mental strength, too. Witch doctors and medicine men put horns on their heads or in their hands. Moses, who received the Tables of the Law from God's hand on Sinai, is often depicted with horns. True, the explanation given is that this is an accident, due to a mistranslation ("with horns") of the Latin word *cornuta*, which should have been rendered as "bright." But it looks like a deliberate mistake, and no one is known to have objected to Michelangelo's horned Moses or to any of the other figures of Moses that Christian art is full of.

Horns and holiness indeed belong together. Some of the earliest Egyptian gods had rams' horns, and they were copied later by some very human "gods," such as Alexander the Great. He is depicted with rams' horns on coins that he had struck after conquering Egypt in 332 B.C. Greco-Roman gods were sometimes represented wearing horns. Among them were Zeus (who also occasionally took the figure of a bull, as when he abducted Europa), Apollo, and Mercury. The same is true of some female deities: Ceres, Diana, and the Great

Moses horned must be one of the best examples known of a mistake that looks deliberate. At any rate there is nothing to suggest that the artist who painted this picture of Moses during the gathering of manna by the Israelites regarded his horns as the result of a mistranslation! Illustration in a 14th-century German biblical manuscript.

Mother, Magna Mater. Bacchus had the appellation "the horned one," and Pan and his attendant satyrs are known by their goats' horns. Perhaps it was due to such gods that Christianity associated horns with "bestiality" and paganism and furnished its enemies, the Devil, Mephistopheles, and other un-Christian demons with horns. The Celts and Teutons also had horned gods. We do not always know their names, but pictures of them have survived in archaeological finds.

The horn's power lay not only in the real, live horns that were borne on their heads by the gods or their earthly equals. It lay also in the discarded, dead horn. Horns were used as receptacles or as musical instruments, but they were sacred. They still had vitality. "Fill thine horn with oil, and go," said the Lord to Samuel when he sent him to anoint David as king of Israel. The "anointing horn" that was used at the coronation of the Swedish king Charles IX in 1606 can still be seen in the royal palace in Stockholm. What happened to the walls of Jericho? "I have given into thine hand Jericho, and the king thereof," the Lord said to Joshua. "And ye shall compass the city, all ye men of war . . . And seven priests shall bear before the ark seven trumpets of rams' horns . . . and the priests shall blow with the trumpets." And when they blew the trumpets of rams' horns, the walls of Jericho fell down.

Not only was the horn sacred in use; its shape was sacred and magical. Sacred goblets were shaped like horns, as were other materials, such as gold, silver, or glass, which were not dependent on the horned shape. Such horns were sometimes used as gifts of an exceptionally exalted character. "And thou shalt make the horns of it upon the four cor-

When the Three Wise Men found their way to the infant Jesus, as related in the second chapter of St. Matthew, they presented gifts. In this picture one of the gifts takes the form of a precious horn. Danish woodcut, 1576.

ners thereof," the Lord commanded Moses when he ordained the structure of the Jewish altar. The Egyptians surrounded their earliest royal tombs with compact rows of bulls' horns, and in Crete large horn-shaped cairns were erected at shrines. Charms to avert evil were (and are) often shaped like horns, and one could protect oneself against "evil eyes" by making the sign of a horn with one's fingers and "butting" with it. Offerings to horned gods, including moon gods (for the half-moon had horns), would be shaped like horns. This was true, for example, of sacrificial bread and cakes. Loaves and pastry shaped like horns are common in many parts of the world; for example, the croissant in France. Is this a final offshoot of horn worship and magic?

The Owl

Looking for a bookstore in a Danish town, we run our eye along the shop fronts and see, among the various other signs, the stylized representation of an owl. This is the bookstore. How can this be? What is the connection between books and an owl? Would not a stork do as well? (And why is it not the owl that brings babies?)

The owl is the bookseller's bird because it was the bird of Pallas Athene, whom the Romans called Minerva. In ancient Greece Athene was the goddess of war; not, it is true, of vulgar fighting (she left that to Mars) but of the art, strategy, and tactics of war. She was also the goddess of the more refined occupations of peace, above all of art and science. She stood for foresight, insight, and wisdom; for studies, learning, and every academic pursuit.

She was the tutelary deity of Athens (the name means "Athene's city"), and her most celebrated temple stood there. Athens was also famous in ancient times for its many owls. They inhabited every part of the town, but particularly the crags and temples of the Acropolis. On some coins of Athens the goddess was shown on one side and an owl on the other. Pallas Athene and the owl came to be closely linked; the owl, as her attribute, came to symbolize the things she stood for: first and foremost wisdom and the pursuit of the sciences and

The *tetradrakme*, the famous four-drachma piece of Athens, from the 5th century B.C. Because of this image the Athenian four-drachma coins were called "owls." On the reverse side was a picture of Pallas Athene, goddess of academic studies. Thus the owl and books came to be associated.

in time every kind of study, student life, teaching, schools, libraries, publishing, and bookselling. The banners of undergraduate bodies often display an owl. Bookends can be shaped like owls. Perhaps the owl's appearance contributed to this. With its forward-looking eyes it almost looks as if it could read, and, when it sits motionless on its branch during the day, it seems to be deep in thought. Clearly the owl is "learned."

Other aspects of the owl have given rise to some quite different symbolism. It shuns the light and only comes to life at dusk. Its element is the night. With its hushed flight and its sinister screech it is popularly thought of as a bird of "ill omen," foreboding death. In art it has stood since the Renaissance for Night and the "children of Night"—Sleep and Death. In the famous plaque by Thorvaldsen on this theme an owl is seen flying behind the genius of Night.

From "darkness" the symbolism was extended to "men of darkness" (e.g., obscurantists), to reaction and pessimism.

This symbolism was developed especially in the Church, which used the owl to symbolize ignorance, superstition, false wisdom, false doctrine, heresy, and those who chose to "walk in darkness" instead of in the clear light of Christianity—that is to say, pagans, Jews, and apostates. An owl could even stand for the Devil. But such is the nature of symbols that at the same time the owl could mean the opposite. Several Fathers of the Church employ the owl as a device for Christ alone in the dark night of agony.

In Denmark this sign indicates a bookseller.

The Stork

Anything in nature that is beautiful or distinctive will engage people's minds. And when it does so it will almost inevitably, sooner or later, be given a "meaning." In other words, it will become a symbol.

That has happened to the stork. Wherever this big, beautiful, trustful bird has lived, it has played a part in legend and fable. This is so in Africa and the Orient, southern Europe, Germany, Holland, and Denmark. It was a pleasure just to see it, and where it settled it brought luck to the family on whose roof it built its nest.

What people particularly noticed was the energy, patience, and care with which the parent storks fed their young. In Hebrew the stork is called *hasidah*, which means "the loving one"; and in the Roman Empire the picture of a stork was employed as an attribute of members of the Imperial house who had been granted the honorary title of Pius or Pia—that is, the pious, the good. It was also thought that young storks later returned their parents' care and affection "when because of old age or sickness they lacked the strength to maintain themselves." The matter is mentioned by a number of classical writers, including Plato, and a Greek law on the obligation of children to maintain their aged parents says expressly, "like the stork."

The stork became a symbol of parental and filial love. From there it was not far to the ruler's love of his subjects and the people's love of their king. But, generally speaking, the mutual love of members of a family, mutual gratitude and appreciation, marital fidelity and fertility, piety and veneration were what the stork stood for. In classical mythology it was associated with Juno and Ceres, the goddesses of marriage and domestic life.

Christianity placed greated emphasis on another aspect of the stork's habits. It is an eater of snakes, thus a serpent killer. And, as the serpent symbolized the Devil, the stork could be enlisted as an image of Christian vigilance and the struggle against evil and of Christ himself. But the Church did not reject classical symbolism outright, and, along with the Renaissance interest in classical antiquity and its ideas, the stork once more became a general symbol of piety.

Perhaps there is a link between the different but kindred ideas of the stork as a bringer of luck, a symbol of mutual family and marital love, and the bringer of babies. When a woman was about to give birth, the other children would be sent out to a neighbor, and, of course, when they returned, they would ask where the baby had come from. It would be

Netherlands printer's mark from the 17th century showing a stork as an image of parental care and affection.

easy to indicate the lucky stork, which, fortunately, was big enough to have carried a swaddled infant in its beak. Where this popular idea originated is uncertain. Perhaps it was in Germany, where the notion of the stork as a bird of good luck has always been especially popular, and where in the 1960s it was chosen as the "national" bird. The explanation or pretext became particularly widespread in the 19th century as a welcome Victorian subterfuge, not least in the United States, where it survived into the present century. Its last refuge seems, significantly enough, to be the Soviet Union, perhaps the greatest stronghold of Victorianism in the world today. At any rate barely a month passes by in which stork-baby jokes do not appear in *Krokodil* or other Russian magazines.

Stork bringing a baby. From an American comic strip, 1903. A number of ladies turn the visitor away, but in the end the main character, the naughty Buster Brown, lovingly accepts both stork and baby.

The Swan

A milk-white swan floating on the water, with the ineffably graceful movements of its neck, is one of the most perfect creatures in nature. Small wonder that men have associated it with all things lovely, above all with women. It was regarded as the bird of Venus, the goddess of love, and symbolized love and lust. But not only that: this spotlessly white bird could also stand for chaste and chivalrous love.

That, however, is not the end of the swan's duality. The bird's turbulent aggressiveness suggested something masculine, an idea that found expression in the story in Greek mythology of Zeus visiting and impregnating Leda in the shape of a swan. "Leda and the swan" came to be one of the commonest erotic themes in art, with the swan as the male. There is something ambiguous, not to say equivocal, about the swan as erotic symbol. It can represent both sexes, simultaneously at that.

This erotic duality is often present in the form of swans or swan disguises in myths and fables. An example is seen in the Valkyris, the warrior maidens of Norse mythology, and their swan transformations. It is suggestive that it was the swan that the romantic, homosexual King Ludwig II of Bavaria took as his personal emblem. He placed representations of swans in hundreds and hundreds of places in his castles, one of which is called Neu Schwanstein (New Swanstone).

But there is also a quite different swan symbolism. The bird was thought to be mute but to speak, or rather sing, once before dying. This is incorrect: the swan is not mute and it does not sing. But the idea must be very old, because the word "swan" seems to mean "singer." The picture of the proud and beautiful bird singing its "swan song," however, has inspired hundreds of generations. Besides Venus the swan was associated with Apollo, the god of music and poetry, and it became a symbol for composers and poets. Ben Jonson called Shakespeare the "swan of Avon." It was no accident that Hans Christian Andersen's ugly duckling was hatched out of a swan's egg. There is a swan on the facade of the academy of music in Brussels, and the institution is called quite simply *Maison de Cygne* (Swan House).

The whiteness of the swan made it a symbol of purity and immaculateness— physically, emotionally, and morally. The picture shows the trademark of a Danish cleaning company.

If the swan symbolized music as well as musicians and composers, surely it could play! French woodcut from the middle 16th century.

The Cock or Rooster

To wake to the sound of cockcrow. Is it not the way life should be? That at any rate is how it used to be for thousands of years for all the people of the earth who kept poultry. It was above all the cock, or rooster, that heralded the new day and proclaimed that the night was over. It was the cock's crowing in the gray dawn that announced the sunrise, the light that put to flight the powers of the night, ghosts and demons, and ended the rule of darkness.

This simple function is the starting point of a tremendous symbolization. The cock came among all cultures to denote alertness and vigilance as well as the light and the sun. The divinities of ancient Greece that personified the sun, especially Helios and Apollo, were often accompanied by a cock, and the same is true of the Norse Heimdal, the watchful guardian of Heaven who seems originally to have been a sun god. To the Romans the cock was associated with Janus, the god of beginnings (it is from him that January, the first month of the year, gets its name). With light and sunshine came fire. The cock was the bird of fire; that was plain to see from its red and golden plumage and flaming comb. The "red cock" was said to crow when a house was on fire. Fire-insurance companies sometimes have a cock in their trademarks.

Of the old religions' symbols there were some that Christianity would have nothing to do with and therefore persecuted and others that it could use and so perpetuated. The cock definitely belongs to the latter group. To the early Christians it was a symbol of the apostles and missionaries, proclaiming the dawn of Christianity after the night of paganism; it stood for the victory of light over darkness and of life over death. The cock became a symbol of the awakening of souls after the last sleep on the morning of the resurrection. That, no doubt, is how the cock on some of the earliest Christian tombs is to be understood.

The cock decorated many an ABC from the 16th to the 20th century. So common was this custom in Denmark that an ABC was called a "cockerel book." The woodcut pictured here is from an ABC printed in Copenhagen in 1591. Perhaps the bird was also intended to remind children to rise early in time for school.

The image was revived in the 16th century when many of the leaders of the Reformation saw themselves as cocks waking the congregations to new life in the "clear light of the gospel" after the spiritual darkness of the papacy. From "light" it was not far to "enlightenment," and the cock came to stand for (Protestant) teaching and instruction. ABC books had a cock on the cover, and this symbol proved to be exceptionally viable. Well into the 20th century there was a cock on the first readers of many European school children. It gradually came to stand for schooling in general and became a school emblem.

From the struggle of the reformers against the Church of Rome and "the black school" it is only a step to the struggle against reaction and obscurantism in a wider connection, and in the 19th century the cock came to symbolize the Press. Many newspapers included a cock in their banner. The cock can also stand for publicity, and a crowing cock represents many advertising agencies. In this sense, however, it can also stem from Mercury, the god of commerce. A cock is one of his attributes, perhaps because he is the messenger and public announcer of the gods.

The new dawn that the cock proclaims can be religious, educational, and intellectual, but it can also be political: for example, the dawn after the long night of colonialism. A cock became the emblem of several of the African liberation movements, and, when Kenya obtained its independence in

The cock announces the dawn of a new day. As a herald and messenger it was also associated with the messenger of the gods, Mercury. The picture shows two cocks drawing Mercury's chariot in a 16th-century German woodcut.

The cock as the symbol of the dawn of freedom—freedom now. The picture was taken in 1961 in Zanzibar; the letters "ZNP" stand for Zanzibar National Party.

1963, the new government put one both in the national arms and in the presidential flag.

But crowing in the morning is not the only characteristic of a cock. At least two others are conspicuous: its strutting and its pugnacity (which are not unrelated). As the British say, it is "the cock of the walk," the boss. It looks after and "serves" a whole flock of hens, a harem, so to speak, waiting on them and being waited on. It was easy to see the cock as a picture of excessive sexuality. When the ten commandments were to be illustrated, in, for instance, the woodcuts, "the poor man's bibles," of the Middle Ages, the cock stood for the sixth commandment, "Thou shalt not commit adultery." In classical antiquity a cock was an attribute of Priapus, the god of reproductive power, and in Christian art it was the symbol of Luxuria, or lust, one of the seven deadly sins. In folk art, e.g., broadsheets, an unfaithful spouse is often shown riding on a cock. Unfairly, a cock was also the mount of the deceived one, the cuckolded husband. The cock could likewise symbolize envy and jealousy. May the occasional depiction of the Devil himself with a cockscomb or feather in his hat be connected with the cock as an attribute of one of the deadly sins?

The cock's aggressiveness and pugnacity are made use of in cockfighting, and this in turn is reflected in our language, "fighting cocks." In Greek and Roman mythology it is an attendant of Mars, the god of war, and in Norse mythology it was the cock that incited the warriors of Valhalla to make war.

But this does not exhaust the activities of the cock as a symbol. Many people will remember from their schooldays the last words of Socrates to his friend Crito before he died: "Remember to sacrifice a cock to Aesculapius." Aesculapius was the Greek god of medicine and healing. He is best known for his serpent, usually twined round a staff. But the cock was also his attribute. The traditional sacrifice from anyone who visited the god's shrines was a cock, perhaps because the temple priests of Aesculapius used the sex organs of castrated cocks as a sort of hormone medicine, which was sold or given out at the temples. At any rate the cock came to symbolize medicine, healing, and rejuvenation. In the 18th-century seal of the Danish College of Medicine there is a figure of Minerva holding a cock in one of her hands.

When Simon Peter offered to give his life for Jesus, the latter replied that before cockcrow Peter would deny him thrice, as he did. The cock is shown here in the courtyard of the high priest between Jesus and Peter.

In Church symbolism one sometimes sees a cock that has nothing to do with the creature as an arouser or herald of a new day. It is the cock that crowed when Simon Peter denied Jesus. The stirring story is told in all four of the New Testament gospels. Jesus says to Peter, ". . . this night, before the cock crow, thou shalt deny me thrice." Though Peter protests, that is exactly what he does. When three different persons at the high priest's palace ask him if he knows the accused, Jesus, Peter says, "I do not know the man." When he said this the third time, the cock crowed. "And he went out, and wept bitterly."

The Gallic cockerel—the French people—together with the rising sun in a French postage stamp.

Through this story the cock became a symbol of Peter's denial and of the apostle himself and also symbolizes human weakness and remorse, together with God's forgiveness.

It is possible that this is the reason why the weathervane on church towers often takes the form of a cock. The custom dates back at least to the 9th century. But the cock's role as the vigilant awakener and herald—of the teachings of Christ and of the Resurrection—would be a sufficient reason. Whatever the explanation, the cock as a weathervane has given rise to a new and separate symbolism. It turns with the wind, and so a cock is a turncoat, a symbol of changeableness, inconstancy, and spinelessness.

And then there is a cock that is quite different from any that has been mentioned. The Latin word for "cock" is *gallus*, which also means "Gaul." The word was a pun even in classical times, and the figure of a cock came eventually to symbolize Gaul and the Gauls. The descendants of the Gauls, the French, adopted the symbol. The Gallic cock, *le coq gaulois*, became popular. It stood for France and the French people: not the French Establishment (that was represented by the royal fleur-de-lis and later by the Tricolor and the Napoleonic eagle) but the "real" France, the people's France. During the French Revolution the cock was incorporated in the banners of the voluntary militia, and it can be seen today on the clothes of French competitors in the Olympic Games.

Yet even the Gallic cock has links with the ones previously mentioned. If, besides "Gaul," *gallus* had also meant, say, "mole," it is not certain that the word play would have become so popular. But the cock, in its red and green iridescent plumage, strutting with curved, pointed spurs and its quivering comb, impaling the sun on its golden cockcrow, is a magnificent fowl. It is proud and self-important, full of fighting spirit and conceit as well as permanently in fine erotic fettle— in short, a creature any Gascon will gladly identify himself with.

And that is perhaps the point. If a thing or a creature is beautiful to look at, if it pleases and cheers, moves, inspires, and uplifts simply by its appearance, it will inevitably become a symbol of, one might almost say, anything. Reasons will be found! They are often merely pretexts. The crucial point is the pleasure of a phenomenon, which can be impossible to define but is no less real for that.

And is that not at least one of the reasons why we humans have been given our intelligence: to subsequently think up intelligent reasons for the actions our impulses and emotions lead us to take?

The Dolphin

Modern science has established that the dolphin is one of the most intelligent of living creatures. At the same time it is a very friendly, indeed affectionate, animal, which, for instance, will help other dolphins that have got into difficulties and will attach itself to human beings in trust and friendship. This last, as well as the dolphin's many-sided talents, can be seen wherever dolphins live in captivity and "perform." It is a moving experience to watch the incredibly graceful animals gamboling in the water and in the air and, totally relaxed, doing their tricks, clearly with the sole object of enjoying themselves and pleasing their human friends.

As in so many other cases it turns out that what modern science has laboriously arrived at was known already—2,000 to 3,000 years ago in ancient Greece. To the Greeks the dolphin was a symbol of intelligence, shrewdness, perspicacity, and prevision as well as of kindness, helpfulness, and friendship. It accompanied ships on dangerous voyages (as any sailor could relate), apparently in order to assist if anything should happen. It carried the drowning and shipwrecked safely ashore on its back. One of those who were saved from a watery death in this way was the famous poet and musician Arion.

On tombstones the dolphin was a common symbol betokening something like: "Love reaches even into the depths." It was the souls' guide; on its back the dead rode to the "happy isles." This picture of a man, a boy, or a child on a dolphin's back as it dances over the waves is one of the finest ever

The dolphin symbolizes speed and zeal, which are appropriate to this 1926 Danish postage stamp.

created. As a symbol it stands for security, unconcern, joy, freedom from care, happiness. From the dolphin as a friend, helper, and rescuer from death and destruction it was not far to "savior," and indeed the dolphin also became a popular symbol among the early Christians. Pictures of dolphins are common in the catacombs of Rome, and there are even examples of Jesus being called "Delphinus."

As a Christian symbol the dolphin gradually died out, but another side of its pictorial power was more lasting. Dolphins, naturally enough, were attendants of the sea god Neptune, and together with him and his trident they came to stand for the sea, the freedom of the seas, navigation, and shipping. In ancient times several Mediterranean trading towns had a dolphin on their coins, as did some maritime or commercial states in later periods. In the late 19th century the copper coins of Denmark bore a leaping dolphin, one of the happiest and most beautiful symbols imaginable.

The Scallop Shell

Aphrodite, goddess of love and fertility, known to the Romans as Venus, was the daughter of the sea. Exactly how she was born was not clear. Some believed that she had sprung from the foam, others that she had come sailing to the island of Cythera in a scallop shell. Foam is hard to draw, whereas a scallop shell, one of the most delightful shapes in nature, is fairly easy to reproduce. So there is no wonder that artists chiefly concentrated on the shell.

The scallop shell was also employed by itself as a symbol of fertility, genesis, life's renewal and prolongation. In the Roman Empire it became a common motif on gravestones, coffins, and tombs, and one or more real scallop shells would often be laid in the grave. They were meant to express the desire for a new life for the deceased and a happy journey until, like Venus on Cythera, he or she arrived on an unknown shore. With Christianity this custom gradually died out, but, strangely, Christianity later adopted a similar one although with a different point of origin. It is not uncommon in Christian graves in Europe to find scallop shells that have been buried with the dead. This is how it came about.

This classical Greek terracotta figure shows Aphrodite sailing in her shell to Cythera. The shell as the attribute of Venus and therefore an erotic symbol may also have had something to do with its resemblance in shape to external female genitals.

When pilgrims in the Middle Ages arrived at the shrine of their destination, they wanted some proof of their having been there. From Jerusalem, for instance, they brought home a palm branch, and at other places they could obtain small figures of the Virgin Mary or a saint. One of the major pilgrimage centers of Europe was Santiago de Compostela in northwest Spain, where St. James, one of the 12 apostles and the patron saint of Spain, is said to be buried. The pilgrims here got a large shell of a distinctive local variety as a pilgrimage "certificate," and this shell soon became so popular that pilgrims to Compostela would put a scallop shell in their hat before leaving home. Inns where pilgrims could spend the night used a scallop shell as a sign, and other places of pilgrimage staked a share in the popularity by taking a scallop shell as their own emblem. The scallop shell became a general symbol of pilgrims, and, when a person who had been on a pilgrimage died, one would be placed in his grave.

But it was not only pilgrims who traveled the roads. The scallop shell was at one time the emblem of vagrants and "knights of the road," and gradually it came to symbolize travel and traveling in general. The Swedish explorer Sven Hedin placed scallop shells in his coat of arms when he was raised to the nobility in 1902, and Cook's travel agency employs one as the firm's emblem. In a sense the wheel has come full circle, and the beautiful scallop shell again means "happy journey!"

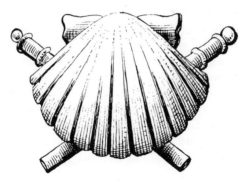

Medieval relief on a French building denoting a pilgrim's inn. Two crossed staffs and a scallop shell are attributes of the pilgrim saint. James and the badge of pilgrims.

The Bee and the Beehive

Man's interest in bees is due above all to their honey. And we are interested in honey because of its sweetness. Of all tastes the sweet is what we like most. Our language indicates this. When we want to say that something is delectable, we have recourse to the sense of taste. "Sweet dreams," "sweet music," "revenge is sweet," "sweet sixteen," "sweet success," "sweet love," "to be sweet on," "sweetness and light," "sweet memory," "sweet spring," "sweetheart."

Honey is the sweetest of all substances. Until the Arabs introduced sugar cane and sugar refining into Europe in the 8th century, it was virtually the only sweetener known there and until the 18th century was still the most important. When God wanted to describe to Moses the attractions of the prom- ised land, he called it "a land flowing with milk and honey." The blissful first days of marriage are called the "honeymoon," in French *lune de miel* and in Spanish *luna de miel*. In the words of the Song of Solomon: "Thy lips, o my spouse, drop as the honeycomb: honey and milk are under thy tongue." "Honey" is a synonym for "darling."

Thus honey symbolized sweetness, in time more particularly "sweet words." The depiction of honey, however, is not easy, and so, to illustrate the idea, recourse was made to bees. One or more bees, perhaps buzzing around a hive, was a symbol in classical times for "fair words," insinuating speech, and eloquence; oratory, rhetoric, persuasiveness. The Muses that had to do with rhetoric and poetry sometimes had bees as their attribute. People who expressed themselves well, either orally or in writing, were portrayed with bees or a beehive. One of these was the Greek historian Xenophon (c. 430–359 B.C.), famous for his "honeyed" style; another was St. Ambrose, Bishop of Milan (c. 340–397), who was depicted with a swarm of bees over his head or a beehive at his side. For this reason Ambrose subsequently became the patron saint of beekeepers.

In his case, howeever, there may have been another factor. His name recalls "ambrosia," the wonderful food of the Olympian gods that gave them eternal youth. Ambrosia was imagined to be a sort of honey, and so bees (or a beehive) came to stand for divine food for the mind, spiritual riches, wisdom, and the word of God.

The symbol of the bee developed new meanings in the Renaissance and later. The "sweet words" were especially regarded as flattery and sycophancy, and persuasive powers came to' mean allurement and seduction. But "sweetness" could also mean "sweetness of character"—gentleness, piety, meekness. The bees assimilated it all, while at the same time the old meanings lived on. Parents who wanted their newborn baby to grow up with irresistible powers of expression smeared its lips with honey, as Anatole France describes in his novel *At the Sign of the Reine Pedauque.*

Title vignette from a 19th-century collection of German poems. For an anthology—the best poems of many writers—the symbol of a beehive, with honey gathered from many places, is well chosen.

Coin from Ephesus in Asia Minor before the birth of Christ, showing the bee of Artemis. The priestesses of the goddess's temple were called *melita*, which might be translated as "honey girls" if this did not produce the wrong associations. In fact, they had to be strictly chaste. How Artemis's chastity could be combined with her role as a goddess of fertility is one of the many riddles of Greek mythology.

Alongside this the bee had also been more obviously employed to symbolize beekeeping. In classical times, for example, a bee was one of the attributes of Ceres, the goddess of agriculture and farm life. It was also associated with Diana, the goddess of hunting and the forest, Artemis to the Greeks; the city of Ephesus in Asia Minor, which was under her protection, had a bee on its coins. Whether the bee of Diana symbolized only the wild honey of the forest or perhaps at the same time something quite different is not easy to decide, however. Diana was also the goddess of chastity, and, apart from the queen and drones, bees are asexual and therefore "chaste." To the Greeks the bee was also a symbol of virginity and sexual purity and thus of the priesthood. Perhaps for the same reason a bee sometimes symbolized the Virgin Mary in the Middle Ages.

Honey, however, is not only a question of *what* but also to a large extent of *how*. It is found in flowers, perhaps one-ten thousandth of an ounce in each, and there, in millions and millions of flights, it is gathered by the bees to be stored in the hive's thousands of hexagonal cells. The process is almost incredible! No wonder, therefore, that it is the starting point of a whole series of symbols.

Above all (in this connection) the bee stands for diligence and industry. The saying "as busy as a bee" seems to go back to ancient Greece. There is a beehive in the state seal of Utah. The bee symbolizes devotion to duty, conscientiousness, perseverance, probity. Medals for "long and faithful service," especially in industry, often display a bee. The busy bee or the whole beehive often symbolizes hard work, enterprise, initiative, and energy, notably in business life. Commercial cities, merchants, and industrialists would include a bee or a beehive in their arms.

The many "little drops" of honey also rendered bees and the hive an obvious model of thrift and saving and in turn, even in classical antiquity, of wealth and prosperity "by joint effort." Savings banks in many countries employ the beehive as a symbol. Bankers' Trust in New York is one example.

Life in the insect state, with tens of thousands of citizens, all in perfect discipline working for the common good under a single supreme ruler, resulted in classical times in the adoption of the beehive as a symbol of "obedience to the sovereign." The Church Fathers took over the image but altered it to mean the Christian's voluntary obedience to God, Christian self-denial, the unity of the believers. In Renaissance symbolism a bee could mean "a subject." At the same time a beehive was the attribute of Concordia, "Concord," and gradually came to symbolize cooperation (under a single leadership). Bees or a beehive were incorporated in the trade- or brand marks of numerous firms.

The Danish savings bank called the Beehive, whose branches have familiar honey-colored frontages, has recently simplified and stylized its original naturalistic beehive symbol and enclosed it in a hexagonal frame, suggesting, of course, the cell of a honeycomb.

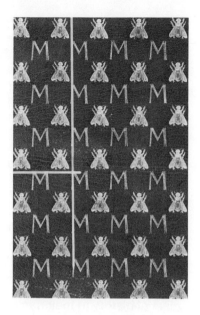

Napoleonic bees used to decorate the binding of a book (shown in detail) that belonged to Mathilde Bonaparte (1820–1904), daughter of Napoleon's brother Jérôme. Royal Library, Copenhagen.

In ancient Rome a beehive also symbolized a *colonia*—that is, a "colony" or new town—founded by ex-soldiers or other settlers, as bees will move from the parent hive to form a new community. The beehive became a symbol for a model community or state or the state pure and simple and thence for the head of state. For example, King Louis XII of France (1498–1515) employed it as a special symbol of sovereignty, with a motto that meant: "The king to whom we bees are subject does not sting." The absolutist kings of the 17th and 18th centuries developed the idea, employing the beehive as a symbol for good government and a well-ordered society, for the mighty but benevolent monarchy that, while it had a sting, did not use it, and that provided honey for all. This simile, of course, was totally false. For one thing, it was not the ruler but the bee people that procured the honey. For another, the bee "ruler" was not a king but a queen, a fact, however, as yet unknown.

More than any other person it was Napoleon who made the bee famous as a symbol for a ruler. During his Egyptian campaign of 1798–99 he had been fascinated by the art of ancient Egypt and its written language, the hieroglyphs.

These had yet to be deciphered, but some progress had been made, and the picture of a bee was thought to mean "king." This was incorrect, though the "bee" sign was part of the written form of the title "King of Lower Egypt." This title may be said to have been "spelt" with a bee. Napoleon, however, assumed that the "bee" stood for "king" or "ruler," and, when he proclaimed himself emperor in 1804, he took the bee as one of his imperial symbols and embroidered it on his imperial cloak, wove it into the cover of the throne, included it in the escutcheons of his marshals, and employed it in scores of other ways.

Through Napoleon himself and his brothers and sisters and descendants, together with the Napoleonic nobility, all of whom exhibited bees wherever possible, bees became a very well-known symbol. Doubtless they came to be seen not only as an emblem of the Bonaparte dynasty but in a wider and vaguer sense as a kind of recognition symbol for other noble but "new" families; that is to say, the sort who had not many years of history to their names but who had risen only recently through their own merits to noble or princely level. At any rate bees or beehives appear throughout the 19th century more frequently than before in the coats of arms of the newly ennobled.

The Signs of the Zodiac

The series of pictures, twelve in all, that is called the signs of the Zodiac is perhaps the oldest collection of living symbols in the world. And living they are! One can scarcely open a magazine anywhere in the Christian world without finding a regular feature, headed perhaps "The Stars this Week" and accompanied by twelve well-known pictures: a ram, a bull, twins, a crab, a lion, a virgin, a balance or pair of scales, a scorpion, an archer (sometimes a centaur with a bow), a goat (perhaps with a fish's tail), a water carrier, and two fishes.

The twelve separate figures are reproduced on medallions or charms by the tens of thousands and in countless numbers on bric-à-brac and souvenirs, on postcards, on capsules and labels, cakes and confectionery. They can be seen on many buildings, both inside and out, in art, on watch and clock dials, and so forth. The signs of the zodiac are probably the most popular and most widely diffused group of pictures in our time.

The original purpose of the twelve devices was to provide a picture of the sun's journey around the firmament in the course of a year, the figures illustrating twelve constellations through which the sun passes in its orbit. Most ancient civilizations formed their ideas of the yearly course of the sun (high in the sky at midsummer, low on the horizon at the winter solstice) and indicated its various "stations" by means of pictures. There were such zodiaclike series of pictures in China, India, Egypt, and possibly among the Indians of South and Central America. Our own zodiac, the one we shall discuss, comes from Babylonian Mesopotamia.

Most of the pictures and names in the zodiac can be traced back to the first flowering of the Babylonian Empire, c. 1900–1700 B.C. Some of them, indeed, can be dated back to the predecessors of the Babylonians, the Sumerians, over 4,000 years ago. As a complete composition, however, the zodiac is probably far more recent, perhaps dating from the 7th or 6th century B.C. In that period the Babylonian Empire experienced a new greatness, and it was probably in the course of the 6th century that knowledge of the zodiac began to spread to neighboring people, among them the Greeks. This process continued in the following centuries. In 538 B.C. Babylon was

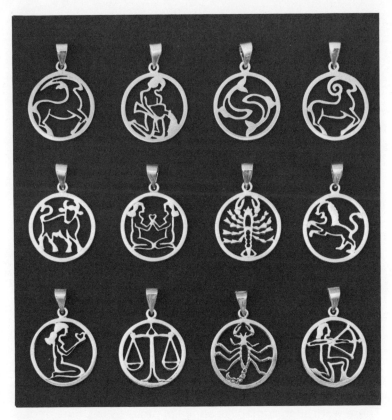

Ornaments showing the twelve signs of the zodiac are produced all over the world in all sorts of materials from the cheapest to the most expensive and in astronomical quantities. This set is in gold. Perhaps because such a medallion is often given as a present, the series begins with Capricorn, belonging to the Christmas month.

conquered by the Persians. Two hundred years later the Persian Empire was overrun by Alexander the Great, and large parts of his conquests were later incorporated in the Roman Empire. Unrestricted communications within these empires meant that Babylonian thought and science were able to scatter their seeds over immense areas. Whether the Babylonians themselves or the Greeks deserve the credit for the complete pictorial form of the zodiac as we know it is a matter of dispute. The oldest surviving reproduction of the complete series, dating from the 5th century B.C., is from Greek territory, and the word "zodiac," "wheel, circle of animals," derives from Greek. It was under this name that the ideas of the signs of the zodiac spread to the whole of the then civilized world.

Over a modern city at night there is a glare of light from street lamps and neon lights, cars and illuminated buildings that makes it impossible to see the stars of the sky. Not many people today have any idea what the firmament looks like and how it "functions," and very few know more than an odd constellation or two. It was different in ancient Babylon. When people took to the flat rooftops in order to breathe freely after the heat of the day, they could see the stars: in fact, they could not help but see them. Through centuries the Babylonians observed the stars in the sky: how the "fixed" stars strode across the firmament in a coherent pattern, thus maintaining their mutual positions; how the "movable" stars, the five planets (all that were known then) together with the moon, moved in altogether different ways, independently of the other stars and of one another. To the most conspicuous stars and groups of stars the Babylonians gave names, drawn from religious and mythological concepts, from terrestrial phenomena they associated with them, or perhaps from what they thought the constellations resembled.

The Babylonian stargazers noticed that besides the usual nightly progress of the fixed stars there was another movement, which extended over many, many nights but in the opposite direction. It was not quite the same pattern of stars they saw every night. To the east more and more of the pattern did not appear, whereas new stars just as gradually emerged in the west. After awhile, however, the familiar stars and constellations reappeared at the exact point in the sky where they had been 365 nights before.

The Babylonians also observed the sun with intense interest. They noticed that its motions were closely connected with the seasons. During one-half of the year, the hot and dry one, the sun rose higher in the sky than in the other, the cold and wet, half. In the first half the days were longer than the nights; in the other half it was the other way around. Twice a year the day and the night were of equal length. And all these phenomena coincided each year with definite positions of certain constellations in the night sky.

The Babylonians observed and took note of, they measured and they calculated, they predicted (rightly) and deduced, and they came to the conclusion that the sun made a vast, circular journey in space around the earth in the course of a year. They also concluded that all life on earth, the changes and variations of nature in the plant and animal world and among men, occurred in correlation with this solar journey. For comprehension and guidance they divided the sun's circular course into a number of equally large sections. There is evidence of early divisions into, among others, eight and ten sections, the eight doubtless because of the quartering of the year indicated by the two solstices and the two equinoxes. But the figure that prevailed was twelve.

The duodecimal division was probably a compromise, the nearest whole figure that could be obtained if the 365 days of the solar journey were to be combined with the moon's periods of about 29½ days (12 × 29½ = 354). The word "month," derived from "moon," suggests that this is what happened. It may also be significant that the duodecimal division is easy to make. The radius of the circle goes exactly six times around in its circumference, as anyone knows who has handled a pair of compasses. The easiest and most obvious way of dividing a circle, therefore, is into six pieces. If this is done twice, starting with two diametrical lines bisecting each other at right angles, the arc, without any calculation or difficulty, will have been divided into 12 equal pieces. At any rate, the sun's yearly course was divided into twelve phases, each twelfth, of course, corresponding to a twelfth of the traveling time.

The figure twelve, as we know, also has arithmetical advantages. It can be divided by two, three, four, and six, and moreover has special relations with eight, nine, and ten. But its specific quality of "completion" or "universality" and therefore something ideal, indisputable, and sublime, doubtless originates from the Babylonian division of the sun's course into twelve phases and hence the year into twelve months. This dividing or grouping into twelve left its mark. The day was divided into twelve hours. There were twelve inches to a foot and twelve pence to a shilling. Israel had twelve tribes, and Jesus twelve disciples. Hercules discharged his twelve tasks; the Romans compiled the twelve tables of the law; a jury consists of twelve persons. We buy sets of twelve, serve for twelve, and give twelve bottles of wine for a celebration.

The Babylonians gave names to the twelve phases of the sun, which were also signs. In most cases they took the name from a characteristic constellation in the relevant part of the sky. In the case of other phases it looks as if the naming was the other way around. Thus it was probably the "watery" period, the Babylonian rainy season of January and February, which gave its name to the part called Aquarius, the water-bearer, the section of the sun's course through which it travels from about January 20 until about February 19. Here, then, terrestrial conditions provided a name for the phase and the constellation. Some of the names of constellations and the corresponding phases still in use can, as indicated, be traced back to the Sumerians, 2,000 B.C. They include Taurus, the bull; Scorpio, the scorpion; Sagittarius, the archer; Capricorn, half-goat, half-fish; and Leo, the lion. Aries, the ram; and Gemini, the twins; are also very old names; Cancer, the crab; Virgo, the virgin; Aquarius, the water-bearer; and Pisces, the fishes, being somewhat more recent. At various times other names were used: Asinus, the donkey, with the crib; Laborus, the laborer; Canis, the dog; Carpentarius, the carpenter; Picarium, the pitcher; Auris, the ear of grain. Libra, the scales or balance, is probably the most recent name.

The twelve signs in general use today are: Aries, Taurus, and Gemini, spring; Cancer, Leo, and Virgo, summer; Libra, Scorpio, and Sagittarius, autumn; and Capricornus, Aquarius, and Pisces, winter. The sequence begins at the spring equinox, about March 21, which is the ancient new year. A remnant of this calendar survives in the names of the months of September, October, November, and December. These months are the ninth, tenth, eleventh, and twelfth of our year, but the names mean "seventh," "eighth," ninth," and "tenth," reckoned from March, the first month of the old year.

As a matter of fact, the observation on which the ancients based their zodiac was incorrect. The sun does not travel around the horizon. It is the earth that moves around the sun, though from the earth it looks as if the sun is moving (in the opposite direction) and that it "leaves" the sign of Virgo and "enters" Libra, and so on. The diurnal and annual "motions" of the sun and fixed stars are illusions, induced by the earth's rotation around itself in the course of 24 hours and its journey around the sun in just over 365 days.

Model of the universe with the girdle of the zodiac, indicating the annual course of the sun through 12 constellations around the firmament. North is at the bottom, as is also indicated by the globe in the middle, which has Europe below Aphri, i.e., Africa. At bottom right is Ptolemy, the most celebrated astronomer of antiquity, and at left, Astrologia, the muse of astrology, as she might be called, shown guiding the seated astrologer. Woodcut title page of Leonhard Reymann's Calendar, Nuremberg, 1515. The picture also shows why we say the tropic of Capricorn and the tropic of Cancer.

To what extent all these astronomical observations had "practical" aims is difficult to say, but at any rate they had practical results. Almost every social activity depends on a division of time and a reliable chronology; and these factors are based in turn on observation of the motions of the sun, moon, and stars (or what look like motions).

The Babylonians, however, had yet another object with their observations and calculations, one that may have been even more important to them. They believed that the celestial bodies exerted an influence on terrestrial life that was decisive to the fate and fortune of every individual. In order to know something about this influence and one's star-determined predispositions and so obtain a guide to one's career and a rule of life, one had to know the positions of the heavenly bodies at the time of one's birth: the phase of the sun (the sign one was "born under") and, above all, where the planets were located in relation to one another and to the other stars.

Fragments of these ancient views are reflected in our language. We speak of "signs in the sun and in the moon" and of being "born under a lucky star." Persons who were under special influence of the moon (Latin *luna*) were considered to be capricious and unstable, from which we get "moonstruck" and "lunatic." Another such word is "saturnine," applied to persons of moody and gloomy temperament who were born under the sign of the planet Saturn. Conversely, anyone born under the sign of Jupiter, or Jove, was merry and convivial— or "jovial."

It is easy to dismiss all this as superstitious nonsense, but in fact good arguments can be adduced for the belief that the celestial bodies influence human life. That the sun does so is obvious (through the seasons and changes in plant and animal life). But there are other and less obvious ways. For example, as the earth's course around the sun does not describe a circle but an ellipse, the earth at certain periods of the year is nearer to the sun than otherwise. This has an effect on terrestrial magnetism, which in turn influences the state of human health, physiology, and consequently psychology. Scarcely anyone will deny that the moon and its motions greatly influence life on earth: it is the cause of tides, whose regular ebb and flow in turn underlie a long range of biological cycles in the plant and

Astrologers believe that the sign that a person is born under and the positions of the planets at the moment of birth exert a vital influence on that person's character and destiny. This woodcut is from the German Jakob Rueff's textbook for midwives, printed in Frankfurt in 1587. In the foreground is the woman in labor; in the background are two astrologers engaged in compiling the newborn baby's horoscope based on the positions of the stars and planets.

animal world, including such a vital fact of human life as female menstruation. In recent times we have gained new knowledge, for example, of cosmic radiation, radioactivity, and ultraviolet rays: influences that come to us from space—that is to say, from stars and planets. Whatever can be adduced for or against astrology, at any rate it has played a very big part in the history of civilization, in religion, philosophy, art, politics, and human daily life.

The Babylonians were concerned above all with the influence of the celestial bodies on the king. It was the position of the signs and the planets in the hour of *his* birth that it was important to know about: for the sake of the king himself but also because the king's life and fortunes were vital to the life and fortunes of the community as a whole. The Babylonians' astrology was if anything an astrology of the state and society.

To the Greeks it was different. To them the influence of the stars and planets on life here on earth meant chiefly their influence on the life of each individual. Everyone was different from everyone else, and this, among other reasons, was due to the influence of the stars. What we call a horoscope—that is, a forecast of important factors or actual events in a person's life based on an exact knowledge of the disposition of the heavens at the hour of his birth—apparently derives from the Greeks.

But it was not only the hour of birth that mattered. By means of a continuing observation of stars and planets the Greek astrologers would predict the weather (which sounds sensible enough) and in turn advise the farmer when to sow, the winegrower when to plant, and the merchant when to travel. They went further. People consulted astrologers about the most favorable time for making a deal and when to sell their house or marry their daughter with the best prospect of success.

In time a comprehensive doctrine of sign reading developed in which sun, moon, the five planets, and the twelve signs of the zodiac were related to very nearly every fact of life: to the human "fluids" and hence temperaments, "humors"; to character, taste, and inclinations, mental and physical aptitudes, work, occupation, appearance, "ages of life" and the seasons; to geographical and climatic conditions, to colors and precious stones, to plants and animals, to sound, light, humidity, drought, heat, and cold.

In order to harmonize all this and prevent one combination or influence from contradicting another, it all had to be carefully "tested." As already stated, it is not quite clear whether it was the Babylonians or the Greeks who devised and elaborated the complete zodiac, but at any rate it was the Greeks who systematized it! It occurred in the 5th, 4th, and 3rd centuries before Christ, and one of the chief architects of the extensive structure was probably the philosopher Eratosthenes (284–204 B.C.).

The success of the zodiac with the Greeks was perhaps partly connected with the fact that its twelve signs were widely associated with episodes, persons, or even gods from Greek mythology. The golden fleece won by Jason was a ram's skin, therefore Aries! And Taurus was Zeus, who changed himself into a bull when he abducted the king's daughter Europa. Gemini were the twin gods Castor and Pollux, also called the Dioscuri. Cancer was the crab that was trodden to death by Hercules, and Leo was the terrible Nemean lion that he choked. Virgo was one of the signs that had earlier had other names, namely Auris. Her period is from about August 23 until about September 23, the harvest time, and she was usually shown holding an ear of corn. It was easy for the Greeks to associate her with their own goddess of agriculture and fertility, Demeter (whom the Romans called Ceres). Virgo, sexually speaking, was no virgin! The period of Libra is from about September 23 until about October 22. Thus it begins at about the autumnal equinox, and that is surely what it denotes: the balance of the day and night. Perhaps it is also a sign of divine righteousness. To the Greeks it could represent either Zeus, who in his capacity of upholder of justice had a pair of scales as his attribute, or of Hermes, whom Zeus usually entrusted to carry them. Scorpio was the scorpion that killed the hunter Orion. Sagittarius was the centaur Cheiron, who taught Achilles to shoot with bow and arrow. Capricorn was the goat Amalthea, which suckled Zeus with its milk. Aquarius was Deucalion, the Noah of Greek mythology and the only survivor of the deluge. And Pisces stood for no less than Venus and Amor (Cupid). Once when they were being pursued by a monster, they flung themselves into a river and were transformed into fishes; and, so as not to lose each other, they tied themselves together with a cord, the way in which Pisces is usually depicted.

Probably in the century after the birth of Christ the Greeks developed another idea that had far-reaching effects. Just as the Jews believed that man was created in God's image, Greek astrologers thought that man was an image of the cosmos. Each of the twelve signs of the zodiac represented a corresponding part of the human body and the energies that resided there. Aries corresponded to the head, Taurus to the neck, Gemini to the arms, Leo to the shoulders, Cancer to the breast, Virgo the stomach, Libra the loins, Scorpio the genitals,

Sagittarius the thighs, Capricorn the knees, Aquarius the calves, and Pisces the feet.

To say that Cancer corresponded to the breast is too noncommittal. Cancer ruled the breast, and the breast obeyed Cancer. That was why the twelve signs of the zodiac governed health and sickness, treatment and cure, life and death. These ideas were accepted by contemporary medical science and developed by the Romans and medieval doctors; they continued to play an important part up to a couple of hundred years ago. Treatment and surgical intervention, such as where a patient's body should be rubbed or oiled and especially where the sick person should be blood-let, depended on the signs of the zodiac.

Bloodletters used to indicate where a patient should be bled according to the sign that he was born under. This 15th-century woodcut has been found in numerous versions almost down to the present day. And if you did not possess such a picture, there was a Latin jingle for memorizing: the shoulder obeys Leo, the breast Cancer; the stomach takes orders from Virgo, the buttocks from Libra; the heat of sex comes from Scorpion, etc.

In the religious practice and social life of the Romans predictions, the reading of omens and the interpretation of natural phenomena, had always been an important factor, and the idea that the disposition of the heavens at a human birth decided that person's character and fate seemed to them trustworthy and reasonable. The zodiac and its ideas were accepted everywhere in the Roman Empire by high and low, and it was the Romans who gave the twelve signs of the zodiac the names by which they are widely known today (even to people who do not speak Latin!).

Each of the twelve signs was regarded as a sort of patron saint of people born in its phase; as their advocates in heaven or in time simply as "month gods." They protected "their" people, and their protégés wore their images as lucky charms. The emperors set *their* zodiac signs for luck on the empire's coins, and Augustus even introduced Capricorn as a standard for the Roman legions. Thousands of signs of the zodiac have survived from Roman times in entire series, e.g., arranged in a circle or on a band or as single figures on trinkets, on medals and coins, in seals and property marks, on private houses and public buildings, in temples and on divine images, on maps and celestial charts, in mosaic floors and on frescoes, on memorial tablets and monuments, on furniture and furnishings of all kinds. The zodiac and its various signs also occur in Roman literature.

One of the nations that were most directly in contact with the Babylonians was the Jewish. In 597 B.C. and again in 586 the Babylonian king Nebuchadnezzar conquered Jerusalem. He transported a large proportion of the Jewish people to Babylon, where they remained until 538 B.C. When the Persian king Cyrus subdued the Babylonian empire in that year, he allowed the Jews to return home.

Babylonian thought and ideas have left numerous traces in the Old Testament, including much evidence of a belief in the influence of the stars on human life. Later, no doubt also influenced by Greek astrology, the Jews became so absorbed by the zodiac that they contravened one of the most important precepts of their religion, the prohibition of images. Some of the oldest and most famous representations of the zodiac derive from synagogues in the Roman Empire.

The belief in stars found in the Old Testament, however, pales into insignificance compared with the account in the New Testament of the birth of Jesus, one of the world's best-known and best-loved stories. In the second chapter of his gospel St. Matthew relates how "wise men from the east" (*i.e.* Babylonian astrologers) came to Jerusalem and asked: "Where is he that is born King of the Jews? for we have seen his star in the east, and have come to worship him." King Herod was appalled when he heard this and, secretly calling the wise men, "enquired of them diligently what time the star appeared." He sent them to Bethlehem, and "the star, which they saw in the east, went before them, till it came and stood over where the young child was."

Despite the words of the evangelist, the Christian church originally rejected all forms of belief in and interpretation of stars and so combated the zodiac. The churchman Origen in the 3rd century sought to ridicule astrology by demonstrating that its astronomical basis was wrong. And Church leaders threatened anyone with penalties who reproduced or wore the signs of the zodiac. It was all in vain. Church opposition, it is true, went on for many hundreds of years, but it was dropped in the end. At the synod of Rome in 799 the Church withdrew its ban on "month images," characteristic scenes of the year's activities, provided that they "reflected reality" (that is, left out the more or less undressed gods of the old Roman pantheon). At the same time it permitted the signs of the zodiac so long as they were seen as "manifestations of God's universal omni-potence." The circle, the band or ring containing the twelve figures, was now interpreted as a symbol of the Creator or of the world itself, of the continuity of life and of eternity. The individual figures were regarded as signs of the month but also as sacred images, as a kind of pictorial stage between earthly and celestial life, between man and God.

Just as the Greeks had fused the twelve signs of the zodiac with their own mythology, something similar occurred with what might be called Christian mythology. Each of the twelve signs was credited with one or more Christian meanings. Here is a list of the commonest. The Ram was the ram Abraham sacrificed in place of Isaac or the Lamb of God, Christ himself.

The signs of the zodiac were stronger than the Jews' ban on images. A number of zodiacs are known from synagogues in Roman times, including this mosaic floor from the 6th century A.D., measuring several meters in each direction, which was excavated in 1929 at Bet Alfa in Palestine. In the middle is the sun, and in the corners the four seasons. From E. R. Goodenough, *Jewish Symbols in the Greco-Roman Period*, vol. 3, 1953.

The Bull was St. Luke the evangelist, whose attribute in art is a (winged) bull. The Twins were Jacob and Esau. The Crab was interpreted as Job and the plagues he was subjected to. The Lion was the prophet Daniel (in the lion's den) or St. Mark the evangelist, whose attribute is a winged lion. The Virgin, of course, was the Virgin Mary. The Scales could stand for the judgment of Solomon or for the prophet Daniel and his celebrated interpretation of the writing on the wall at the feast of Belshazzar: "Thou art weighed in the balances, and art found wanting." The Scorpion could be King Rehoboam, who said: "My father hath chastised you with whips, but I will chastise you with scorpions." The Archer was either Ishmael, who "dwelt in the wilderness, and became an archer," or Nimrod, who "was a mighty hunter before the Lord." The Goat was interpreted inter alia as Aaron: "And Aaron shall bring the goat upon which the Lord's lot fell." The Water Carrier, of course, was John the Baptist! And the Fishes could be either Jonah, who was swallowed by a whale, or Jesus, who performed the miracle of the loaves and fishes. Because of their number the twelve signs were also frequently equated with the apostles or other groups of twelve (prophets, patriarchs).

From the 12th century the signs of the zodiac were common in church decoration. In the 13th century the scholastic philosophers began to interest themselves in astrology. Scholasticism sought to combine Christian theology with classical philosophy and science. It was also influenced by Jewish and Arab philosophers, and the schoolmen found information and ideas about the zodiac in all of these. The result was a philosophical compromise. Stars and planets, they argued, are God's tools and as such can influence life on earth. Man can accept the influences of the stars, their "inclinations," or reject them. In any case the heavenly bodies work only on men's bodies, not on their souls.

This interpretation, of course, gave impetus to the doctrine of the dependence of the human body and human health on the heavens, a doctrine that now became almost "official." There were astrologers at the courts, at the universities, and in observatories. Scarcely a calendar was made that did not include the twelve signs of the zodiac. The zodiac had been promoted to a "chair." No one any longer wanted to reject St. Matthew's story of the star. The wise men from the East and the star that led them to the birthplace of Jesus had become one of the most popular subjects of Christian art. In painting and sculpture, in prose and poetry, the Star of Bethlehem developed into one of the most vital images of Christian symbolism.

The Renaissance "rediscovery" of Greek and Roman antiquity added more fuel to the fire of astrology. In the 16th and 17th centuries hardly anyone, from the most ignorant to the most learned, doubted that the zodiac and the planets exerted a vital influence on every human life. For every human act—in war and peace, in commerce, art, and love—there was a most favorable moment, and it could be arrived at by a study of the heavens. Every princely court had its astrologer. Renaissance and baroque writing and art, even architecture, are permeated with astrological motifs, metaphors, and proportions. Much of this can rightly be understood and appreciated only through a knowledge of contemporary astrological ideas.

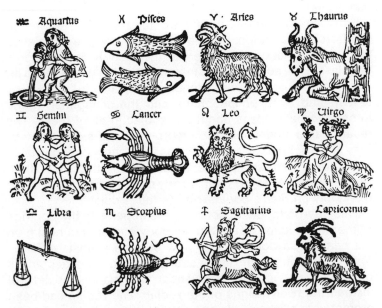

Astrologers in preparing their horoscopes gradually developed a number of abbreviated symbols for the 12 signs of the zodiac and their names. Some of these may date back to antiquity; others are much more recent. But by the 15th century all 12 were fixed. In this woodcut illustrating pictures of the months from a German calendar c. 1500, the signs are shown with the corresponding pictures and their Latin names. Most of the signs have developed from abbreviations of the respective names, usually in their Greek form. At the same time a number of the signs seem to be meant to "resemble" the picture they represent or part of it: for example, Pisces, Taurus, Libra, and the bow of Sagittarius. At least one of the signs, Cancer, stems from Arabic astrology.

The fact that the firmament was also studied and explored scientifically in those centuries made little difference to the acceptance of astrology. Astronomers—Tycho Brahe, for example—were usually astrologers themselves. In the 18th century the Enlightenment probably reduced the number of believers in astrology but not noticeably. The first printers in North America had only a rudimentary range of type, but the twelve signs of the zodiac had their place in every lettercase. Among other applications they were employed in draft designs of the first bills for the United States around 1776. The romantic age displayed an interest in and sympathy for the zodiac, and in our own century it has experienced a new, tremendous wave of popularity. Sometimes its adherents bring forward the latest knowledge about the forces of the universe in its defense, but this in fact is mistaken as well as superfluous. The zodiac does not base itself principally on physical realities but on psychological ones.

Whether all these people over the last 3,000 to 4,000 years, from the most ignorant and superstitious to the most intelligent and most learned men of their time, from the most anonymous to the rulers of the world—the Emperor Augustus, Gustavus Adolphus, Hitler—whether all these people actually believed in astrology is impossible to ascertain. Some undoubtedly did. Some perhaps partly; sometimes and sometimes not. Others again may have been attracted by the ingenious and beautiful complex of ideas and have wanted to be able to believe in it.

A few years ago I met a man, rather older than myself, shrewd, traveled, experienced, who told my fortune. He studied my palm and from its lines foretold that I would grow old but would not be ill and that I would die abroad. I do not believe it. But I have not been able to forget it. The two forecasts fascinate me. And perhaps I shall end up by believing them.

One might recall an anecdote about the Danish nuclear physicist Niels Bohr. A horseshoe hung over the door of his country cottage. A visitor exclaimed: "You, a great scientist, surely can't be superstitious! Surely you don't believe in that!" Bohr replied: "Well, I don't. But I've been told that a horseshoe brings good luck even though you don't believe it!"

The fact that belief in the signs of the zodiac has survived and still flourishes, that it has almost been strengthened by the criticism of science, the hostility of Christianity, and the ridicule of the Enlightenment, is in my opinion largely due to the *imagery* of the zodiac, the twelve figures that constitute the system's visual basis.

Human history, political as well as intellectual—the history of thought, religion, and science—is full of world schemes and world views, of theories, doctrines, systems, explanations, and philosophies, that are at least as feasible as the zodiac but that have been completely forgotten. The 4,000-year-old zodiac, however, is one of the most familiar of modern phenomena. Opinion polls in America and Europe have shown that virtually everybody asked knew the sign they were born under. "I am Libra! I'm Aquarius!" The *image* has a power that is not normally realized.

In the first place this is presumably due to purely physiological factors; namely, the fact that vision is man's predominant sense. To other creatures, for example, the dolphin and the bat, hearing is the most important sense; to others again, e.g., the dog, it is smell. But to man it is the gift of sight that is the all-important factor in our conception of the outside world and

The week's horoscope given in popular magazines is nothing new. This is a general horoscope for the year 1487, month by month, in a calendar printed by Konrad Kachelofen in Leipzig.

It was in the months of March, April, May, and June (1845) that Ecuador revolted against Spain and gained its independence. To commemorate these four months, the corresponding signs of the zodiac, Aries, Taurus, Gemini, and Cancer, were incorporated in the country's national arms.

our opinion of it. "I see," we say when we *understand* something. A dog would say, "I smell." "As I see it," "in my view," means "I think" or "I believe." A person who has abnormal powers of perception and can "see" into the future is said to have "second sight." Language teems with expressions like "see to," "see into," "see about," "insight," "oversight," "see" the truth. What we see with our eyes registers more strongly than any other impression.

Added to this biological lead is the fact that a picture is so uniquely practical. Visual communication and imagery are far older than written languages—and will no doubt survive them! Pictures impart their message regardless of the spectator's language, linguistic knowledge, or ability to read. Some pictures mean what they represent—the picture of a telephone on the door of a telephone booth, for example. They can be useful but do not give much flight to the imagination. Symbols, which mean something different from what they represent, do. And as far as meaning something different is concerned, the signs of the zodiac are unrivaled!

As a unified composition—for example, in a circle, a ring, or a belt—the twelve signs stand for the sun's course, for the firmament and the heavens, for the "world entire," for the universe, the cosmos. They can stand for the astronomical sky but also for the metaphysical or theological, the abode of the blessed. The twelve signs can stand for the Creator, God. In the Roman Empire they also came to symbolize the emperor and hence "the Roman peace" and the golden age that the *Pax romana* had brought about. But the series in addition represents a year, the year's course and the course of years, time and passage of time, eternity. And through this it can further symbolize existence, human life, fate, life and death, "full circle," the continuing cycle of nature: the permanence of nothing but the return of everything.

Singly the twelve signs illustrate a twelfth of the sun's course and a twelfth of the corresponding travel time, the period from about the 21st of one month to about the 21st of the next; or they mean simply a month, the one in which the period starts. The twelve signs can further represent anything that has occurred in their period: a human birth (perhaps its commonest function) or some other crucial event—say, a wedding, a victory, a lucky turn of fortune—which surely explains why the Emperor Augustus took Capricorn, the sign for December, as his device, though he was born on September 23 (another theory is that Capricorn represents the date of his conception). The twelve signs did service as month symbols for many centuries in practically every almanac in Europe. They served a similar purpose as date stamps on the products of gold- and silversmiths; in Denmark, for example, on all works of gold and silver from 1685 to the second half of the 19th century.

From these symbolizations of space and time the scope of the twelve signs was extended, as we have seen, to an almost incredible degree. They can stand for virtually every human psychological and physiological potentiality: for characteristics, temperaments, dispositions, inclinations, ambitions, feelings, emotions, health and sickness, bodily organs and functions, mental aberrations. Furthermore, for wind and weather, temperatures, color, seasonal variations, all the changes of earthly life, and so on almost ad infinitum. It is the function of symbols to express the abstract by means of the concrete, and it is a function that the signs of the zodiac perform better than any other symbols one can think of. They can be employed singly, in combinations of two or more, or all twelve together—a number that fits every shape and every design: the circle, square, oblong, triangle. They are simple, easily understood and recognized, and beautiful. As visual symbols they are without equal.

Along with these "practical" advantages, however, there is at the same time a deep psychological satisfaction. To "translate" the intangibles of space, time, and the human mind into something as tangible and "understandable" as a picture of a ram, a pair of scales, or two fishes meets a tremendous psychological demand. We all yearn to understand. The simplifications of the zodiac render the incomprehensible comprehensible and the unintelligible intelligible. The twelve signs of the zodiac "explain" space and time and life, making us feel that we understand everything.

There is yet another psychological satisfaction in the signs of the zodiac: the identification that they offer us. One of the functions of the signs of the zodiac is to represent or characterize the people who have been born under the respective sign. As we have all been born under one of them, it follows that the zodiac gives to everyone in the world a picture identity, a psychological and visual affiliation; if you like, a device and a totem. Why this is so important can be hard to explain, but that it is no one can doubt who sees the signs displayed hundreds of times a day by all sorts of people on necklaces, bracelets, and rings, as transfer pictures on motorcycles and cars.

The fact that the series is called "zodiac," meaning "wheel, circle of animals," though only seven of the twelve are animals, is no accident. The role of animals in the world of symbolism overshadows that of every other group, and, in order to explain this, it is not enough to talk of man's interest in or love of animals. It is an emotion that goes far deeper. From the earliest times men have called themselves Wolf or Horse. Popes and kings called themselves Lion (Leo) or Lionheart. In Scan-

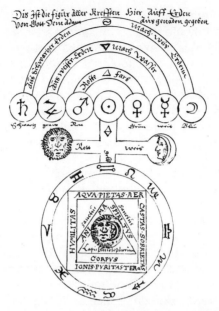

The circle below is a zodiac with abbreviated signs instead of pictures. Inside it is the square of the four elements, inside that the human triangle (body, mind, and soul), and inside that in turn, in the shape of the combined sun and moon, the object of it all, the Philosopher's Stone, *lapis philosophorum*. Above are the signs of the sun and moon, and above them the signs of the seven planets: Saturn, Jupiter, Mars, the sun again, Venus, Mercury, and the moon again. Diagram in an alchemical manuscript c. 1580.

dinavia the aristocracy took names like Ox, Falcon, Boar, Doe, Crab, Beetle, Pike, Porpoise, Hawk, Lark, and the middle classes followed suit with Stork, Crane, Mouse, Raven, Plover, Swan, Lion, Mare. Nowadays we have all sorts of group names: Cub Scouts, Desert Rats, and Black Panthers. From primeval hunting magic to present-day advertising ("Put a tiger in your tank!") our world is full of the idea that animals are ideal. We would like to be like them. We would like to *be* them! And so at many a party in 1978 you will hear people say, "My husband is Aries, and I'm Leo."

All this—the advantage of the visible, the practical advantages, the psychological satisfactions, the assurance of identification and of course the aesthetic pleasure—combines in the delight of a picture its fascination and its power The zodiac is irresistible. Irresistibility, however, has its risks. The more popular a symbol, the more frequently, of course, it is used. And the more frequently it is used, the more it is in danger of losing its symbolical significance and ending up as a mere embellishment, a pretty decoration, to be sure, but without meaning. The rose—the rose of love, passion, intimacy, and friendship—becomes a rosette, an ornament. The palm branch of victory, triumph, honor, and martyrdom ends as the palm in a decorative medal. The zodiac is well on the way to this. Its signs appear where they have neither meaning nor function, for instance, on apartment blocks or any sort of monument.

It was mentioned earlier that the zodiac was built on a wrong foundation, because it is not the sun but the earth that makes a yearly journey in space. This fact was known in classical times and again in the Renaissance without making the slightest difference to the spread and popularity of the zodiac. There is, however, another factor that one might think would challenge belief in the zodiac and astrology to a far greater extent.

Besides revolving around itself and around the sun, the earth moves in yet another way. It tips in a circulatory motion, rather like the lid of a pan when it comes to rest on a kitchen table. The earth's axis, the line from pole to pole around which it rotates, does not always point in the same direction. It was thought to do so, and this apparent constancy gave rise to a particular symbolism. For the past thousand years or so the earth's axis has been pointing (almost exactly) toward the Pole Star. From the earth it looks as if the Pole Star is the only point in the sky that does not move; while everything else seems to move, the Pole Star remains immovable at the same point in space. Of course, the Pole Star "rotates" along with all the other stars (or, rather, it does not rotate any more than any other of the fixed stars do; they only seem to rotate). This immobility has created great respect for the Pole Star. It has been praised in poetry and has become a symbol. A Swedish order has been called after it, and the motto of the Order of the North Star is *Nescit occasum* ("It knows no setting"). It is consant; one can steer by it; it can be trusted.

All this, however, is an illusion, due to the fact that the

A fine specimen of the zodiac consists of the two circles, each containing the twelve signs, in the famous astronomical clock in the cathedral of Lund in Sweden. It dates from c. 1400 (though much restored later). At the top is a planetary clock with a movable zodiac circle, and below (pictured here) a zodiac enclosing a calendar up to the year 2123. In the top right-hand corner between Cancer and Leo the sun can be seen on its course around the circle.

circular motion of the earth's axis is so very slow, requiring about 25,800 years to get around to the same point. From the earth, of course, it appears as if it is the sighting point of the earth's axis *and the whole of the rest of the sky* that rotate (in the opposite direction) in the course of 25,800 years. If we divide the 25,800 years of this (apparent) revolution between the twelve phases of the sun, we get about 2,150 for each. That is to say that the sun, if observed on a definite day of the year, say, the spring equinox, will gradually in the course of about 2,150 years get as a "background" a different one of the twelve constellations.

In the 2,150 years from about 2340 B.C. to about 190 B.C. the sun at the vernal equinox, March 21, was in the zone of Aries. From about 190 B.C., observed as March 21, the sun moved into the neighboring phase of Pisces, and it moved within the limits of this zone in the following 2,150 years until about 1960. Each year from 1960 until about 4110 the sun on March 21 will be in the zone of Aquarius. And before entering Aries in about 2340 B.C. it had, from about 4490 B.C., moved through Taurus (apparently, since it is still the earth that moves).

The astronomical limits between the zones have not, however, been accurately determined, and consequently the above chronological intersections cannot be either. The *length* of the periods is fixed at about 2,150 years, but the calculations of the beginning and ending of the periods can vary by several hundred years.

The discovery of the 25,800-year rotation of the earth's axis was made by a Greek astronomer, Hipparchus, in c. 130 B.C., and already at that time the names and signs of the zodiac, starting in Aries from March 21, did not correspond with the astronomical facts: as stated, from about 190 B.C. the sun had no longer been in the sign of Aries at the vernal equinox but rather in Pisces. And since then Pisces has also slipped past the sun, which on March 21 each year is in the sign of Aquarius. At any rate, we can deduce from this that the zodiac system cannot be older than about 2340 B.C. The system's annual point of departure at the vernal equinox is Aries, and it was not until about 2340 B.C. that the sun was in the sign of Aries at the equinox.

The astonishing thing is that the system has survived this

disparity between its original basis and the current physical reality and that it is still going strong. The discovery by Hipparchus was common knowledge in antiquity. Origen refers to it in his previously mentioned attack on astrology. But it clearly made not the slightest impression on the millions and millions of people who from about 190 B.C. sought and still seek information and help from the zodiac that the entire firmament was dislocated, first by one phase and then, from about 1960, by a second and that the constellations and the corresponding signs of the zodiac no longer coincide. If your birthday falls between March 21 and April 22, you will say that you were "born in the sign of Aries." This may be astrologically correct, but it is astronomically wrong. If you were born before 1960, you were born under the sign of Pisces; if you were born after 1960, you were born under the sign of Aquarius.

On the contrary, the dislocation has given rise to new symbolical interpretations. We speak of the "eras" of Taurus, Aries, Pisces, and Aquarius, 2,150-year periods supposed to show a connection with the creature whose name they bear. The Taurus era, c. 4490–2340 B.C., according to this interpretation, was characterized by the cult of the bull, e.g., Apis, the Minotaur; the Aries era, c. 2340–190 B.C., by the cult of the ram, e.g., Amon. The Pisces era largely coincided with the supremacy of the Christian religion, as a fish from the start was a symbol for Christ and Christianity. Aquarius, from c. 1960, is supposed to symbolize "what lies ahead" (space research, for example), the advancing and accelerating, the revolutionizing and revolutionary. The next 2,150 years will show whether this applies.

The image is greater than reason. It is more powerful than the testimonies of science and the exhortations of religion. It is no accident that Judaism, Islam, and Christianity (if the ten commandments are to be taken seriously) forbid any form of imagery: "Thou shalt not make unto thee any graven image, or any likeness of any thing that is in heaven above, or that is in the earth beneath, or that is in the water under the earth . . . for I the Lord thy God am a jealous God." Images can indeed make people forget what the Lord would have them believe.

The English King Stephen (1135–54) was a grandson of William the Conqueror. When his uncle died in 1135, he laid claim to the English throne, succeeded in gaining power, and was proclaimed king. All this took place in the period of Sagittarius, and for that reason the sign of Sagittarius, the arrow-shooting centaur, became associated with Stephen. Whether he himself adopted the sign or others assigned it to him is not clear. The centaur's lion body was no doubt due to the influence of the traditional three lions of the English royal arms.

Fabulous Animals

The Phoenix

The badge on the young man's blazer showed a beautiful and fascinating figure: a golden bird with spread wings rising from red flames. What was it? What did it mean? It was the Phoenix, he explained, and he said it was his college badge.

The Phoenix is a fabulous creature with an ancient history. It is mentioned in ancient Egypt, in the Book of Job, by the Greeks and Romans, and by the Arabs. In appearance it is not very extraordinary. The Greek historian Herodotus, who lived in the 5th century B.C., describes it thus: ". . . its plumes are partly golden and partly red, and in size and appearance it bears most resemblance to an eagle." The things that make the Phoenix exceptional are quite different.

For one thing, there is never more than one in the whole world. For another, it lives to an immense age; 540 years, the Roman Pliny believed according to Semitic tradition a thousand years. When it feels that its time is up, it builds a nest of spices in the desert from rare trees and, by flapping its wings, sets fire to the nest and burns itself to death. But then (the vital point!) the Phoenix rises again from the ashes to new life.

The phoenix rises from the ashes to a new life, as shown here in the headpiece of an Italian book published in 1494. In Greek the word *phoenix* also means "palm" and may be connected with Phoenicia, meaning perhaps "Land of Palms." Did the phoenix originate there?

In antiquity the Phoenix symbolized long life, agelessness, and eternity. To Christianity it became first and foremost a symbol of the Resurrection and eternal life; indeed it was an argument for these things. "Should men perish, when the Arabian bird is sure of resurrection?" the churchman Tertullian asked c. 200.

Its capacity for rebirth was the Phoenix's reward for having been the only creature in the Garden of Eden to resist Eve's temptation to eat of the Tree of Knowledge. So it also became a symbol of steadfastness in the face of temptation, of chastity and other Christian virtues, of the Virgin Mary and her immaculate conception, and of Christ himself.

Alchemists employed the Phoenix as a symbol for fire (one of the four elements); and, when it stood for resurrection, rebirth, or renewal, it was often in association with fire. Many fire-insurance companies all over the world are named Phoenix.

In the early 18th century the old college at Sorø in Denmark languished, but in 1747 it was revitalized, and at the same time a Phoenix was included in its badge. The symbolism of the badge was reinforced when the college burnt down in 1813 but actually rose again from its ashes. The boys are fully entitled to the Phoenix they bear on their badges and buttons.

Symbols, however, can also be abused. No tourist in Greece in the early 1970s could avoid seeing the Phoenix devices, often backing a soldier in field dress, that were displayed, painted, or carved all over, and were also shown on the country's postage stamps. It was the government of Colonels advertising itself and the "rebirth" of the Greek nation signified, in their own view, by their coup.

In June 1973, Papadopoulos introduced the yellow Phoenix rising from red flames against a blue background as the arms of Greece and displayed it inter alia on his own flag as self-appointed president. In November of the same year, however, he was overthrown, and later the same fate overtook his killers. The Phoenix will probably be compromised as a device in democratic Greece for many years to come.

The Sphinx

The fabulous creature called the Sphinx symbolizes, first and foremost, mystery, secrecy, silence, inscrutability, and the riddle of the universe and secondarily divine and human wisdom, sagacity, discernment, and temperance. The Sphinx also stands for the particular riddle some men believe woman to be: the mysterious, cruel, fateful femme fatale or man-eater and

This is the Sphinx, with a definite article and a capital S, as there is only one. It is the Greek Sphinx, shown with the face of a woman, seated and winged. The mountain that it inhabited was near Thebes in Boetia. Painting on a Corinthian drinking vessel.

hence for erotic obsession and inexorable sexuality. How can they go together: temperance and erotic obsession, discernment and mysteriousness?

The explanation is that the European Sphinx is an amalgam of two widely differing fabulous creatures. The Sphinx of Greek mythology was a monster with the head and breasts of a woman, the body of a lion, and the wings of an eagle. It inhabited a mountain, where it asked every passer-by a riddle. When they failed to solve it—which they always did—they were strangled (the word *sphinx* probably means "strangler"). One day, however, King Oedipus of Thebes arrived. He gave the right answer to the riddle, whereupon the Sphinx slew itself.

When the Greek historian Herodotus visited Egypt in the 5th century B.C., he took the colossal statues of lions with human heads that he saw there to be a form of Sphinx, and that was what he called them. In Egypt, however, they were called something quite different, and they represented something quite different. They were "images of majesty": the head of a

At the royal hunting lodge of Eremitage in the woods north of Copenhagen, built 1734–36, there are four sphinxes, but what they are meant to symbolize, if anything, is hard to say. The mysteries of nature? The erotic possibilities of an outing to the woods? Or are they a symbol of sovereignty, flanking the entrance to the royal palace, like the royal grave in their Egyptian homeland?

king or a god, wearing a royal headdress, combined with the body of a lion. The head was nearly always that of a man, and the figure was always shown lying down, unlike the Greek Sphinx, which was female and generally shown seated. The Egyptian figures were meant to express the might, dignity, intelligence, and strength of Pharaoh.

The Sphinx became common in European art in the Renaissance and later, depicted most often wingless, with the woman's head and breasts of the Greek Sphinx on the recumbent lion's body of the Egyptian. And, just as the appearance was a mixture, so too the symbolism: the erotically tinged cruelty of the Greek Sphinx was combined with the eternal meditation of the desert Sphinx.

To Danes and Norwegians the Sphinx is particularly interesting in that the Danish-Norwegian author Ludvig Holberg used it as his emblem; two sphinxes flank the coat of arms he was granted when he was made a baron in 1747. Several of the characteristics or ideals represented by the Sphinx might be called Holbergian: e.g., discernment, reflection, and temperance. He gave no indication of the reason for his choice, but perhaps the omission was in keeping with what his sphinxes were meant to express. "Silence was to his taste," it has been said of Holberg, and silence was exactly what, among other things, the Sphinx stood for.

Pegasus

The winged horse Pegasus is unquestionably one of the best-known symbols. Everybody knows what it stands for: poets and poetry, from the most sublime to the most primitive jingling. Possibly its popularity has something to do with the slightly comic sound of the word. Pegasus!

Pegasus derives from Greek mythology and originally its connection with poetry was only secondary. It was begotten by Poseidon, the god of the sea, the counterpart of the Roman Neptune, and the horrifying female creature Medusa. When the hero Perseus slew Medusa, Pegasus sprang from her

The spring of poetic inspiration wells forth where Pegasus strikes the mountain with its hoof. Seated at the foot of the mountain are the nine muses. French publisher's mark from the beginning of the 17th century.

blood. Later it became the mount of another hero, Bellerophon, whose exploits, performed with the help of Pegasus, made him arrogant. Setting course for Mount Olympus, the home of the gods, he provoked the wrath of Zeus and was thrown from his winged horse and dashed to death. Pegasus then became the mount of Zeus.

In the state religion of Rome Pegasus bore the dead emperor to the land of the dead. In time others too made the journey to the beyond on the back of Pegasus. Its image is found fairly often on contemporary tombstones. The Middle Ages and Renaissance dwelt particularly on one episode in the life of Pegasus. Once it visited the nine Muses in their home on Mount Helicon, and, where it struck the rock with its hoof, a spring gushed forth whose waters were poetically inspiring. Whoever drank of Hippocrene, as the spring was called, became a poet.

Through this story the winged horse came to symbolize poetic gifts and the art of poetry and to some extent the Muses' other "official" spheres: drama, music, history, and the rest. It is easy to understand the symbol's triumphal progress. Surely the beautiful, fabulous horse itself was an image of the idea that soared aloft on wings of poetry!

The Unicorn

Of all the fabulous beasts created by the human imagination, the unicorn is perhaps the most phenomenal: in its wild beauty it is the most magnificent and at the same time the one that most powerfully satisfies man's need of symbols.

The first to mention the unicorn was the Greek doctor Ctesias, who wrote about 400 B.C. He said that it lived in India and that it was greatly prized because its horn had the wonderful property of neutralizing all kinds of poison. A drinking cup and platter of unicorn horn are a guarantee against poisoning. Consequently, rulers were ready to pay anything for this horn.

Later authors embroidered the theme. The unicorn could cleanse polluted drinking water by making the sign of the cross in it with its horn. No other animal and no hunter could match it in strength and swiftness. The unicorn was untamable, and there was only one way of catching it. A young virgin

The unicorn resembles a slender horse, but with cloven hooves and usually a goatlike beard. Above all, however, it is recognizable by its magnificent horn. It is generally white, with a golden horn and golden hooves. A 17th-century German woodcut is shown here.

had to sit in the forest, and the unicorn would then come and lay its head in her lap and fall asleep.

This story was interpreted by the Christians in the sense that the unicorn was Jesus, who, on being taken to the Virgin Mary, entered her womb to be borne by her. The theme was wide-

Unicorn cleansing a polluted spring. Renaissance Italian woodcut.

spread. The hunting of the unicorn and its being driven to the virgin's lap were an image of the conception of Jesus. Slaying the unicorn was an image of Christ's crucifixion and death.

The sexual associations naturally connected with the unicorn's horn and the beautiful, ambivalent story of the virgin in the forest also made the unicorn an erotic symbol. For centuries it was an indispensable part of the decoration on bethrothal chests and other sweetheart's presents, where it appeared in innumerable graceful situations. Alongside this the unicorn discharged its original task of revealing poison and cleansing drinking water. It personified purification, antidotes, cures, and medical science. Both in Europe and in the New World it became a common sign of doctors and especially chemists. It can still be seen in many places in this last capacity.

The unicorn frequently occurs in heraldry: for example, as a shield-bearer of the kings of Scotland or Great Britain (shown here). From heraldry the beautiful and mysterious animal spread to many other fields from inn signs to nursery rhymes.

Man

A number of European cars have chosen as their emblems the arms of the cities where they are made. The Ford Taunus, for example, uses the arms of Cologne (whose three crowns stand for the three wise men, who are buried in Cologne); the Volkswagen has the arms of Wolfsburg, the wolf and castle; and Morris, the arms of Oxford, the ox at the ford. The group also includes the Alfa-Romeo, the famous Italian car. It is made in Milan, and its emblem incorporates two devices representing that city: a red cross on a white ground (the actual city arms) and a creature resembling a serpent or a dragon that is swallowing a human being. The latter device is the coat of arms of the celebrated noble family of Visconti, who ruled in Milan from the 13th to the 15th century. There are various explanations and interpretations of this distinctive and disturbing heraldic device, some historical, others religious or magical, all imaginative and all wrong. What follows is probably the right one.

In the first centuries of Christianity man already thought of interpreting episodes or events in the Old Testament as a sort of prototype or prefiguration of episodes or events in the New Testament, regarding the Old Testament to a wide extent as a prophesy of the real, the New, Testament. Abraham about to sacrifice his son Isaac was seen as a prefiguration of the crucifixion of Christ; Jacob's ladder was interpreted as a prefiguration of Christ's ascension; the rain of manna in the wilderness as a prefiguration of the Last Supper, and so on.

In the visual art of antiquity and especially the Middle Ages these prefigurations were very widespread. The reason may partly have been that men long hesitated to depict Jesus himself and the sacred scenes surrounding him, but probably even more important was the fact that in many cases the prefigurations made it possible to illustrate something abstract by means of something concrete. One of the most popular of all prefigurations was the prophet Jonah. In order to abate the storm, he was thrown overboard by his shipmates and was swallowed by a "whale." "Then Jonah prayed unto the Lord his God out of the fish's belly . . . And the Lord spake unto the fish, and it vomited out Jonah upon the dry land."

Perhaps in the 13th century the story of the miraculous deliverance of Jonah made such an impression on a member of the Visconti family that he took the theme for his coat of arms (left). From the Viscontis the emblem passed to the city of Milan, and from the city to the car factory.

Scenes from this superb story were depicted again and again. Jonah being thrown into the sea was equated with the betrayal of Jesus; Jonah in the monster's jaws, with Christ's descent into Hell or, more likely, his resurrection. The amazing part of the story indeed was not that Jonah was swallowed or that Jesus died but that Jonah came unharmed out of the fish's belly and that Jesus rose again from the dead.

And no one could challenge the story's symbolic authority, for Jesus compared himself several times with Jonah: for example, in Matthew 12:40: "For as Jonas [New Testament spelling] was three days and three nights in the whale's belly; so shall the Son of man be three days and three nights in the heart of the earth." And that is what the Visconti and Alfa-Romeo devices represent: not a serpent swallowing a child but a "whale" vomiting out Jonah unharmed. It is a symbol of God's intervention on behalf of the believer, of salvation, resurrection, and eternal life.

Left: Samson breaking through the gate of Gaza. Right: Jonah being spewed out of the mouth of the whale. Middle: what both images prefigure, Jesus breaking open the tomb to rise from the dead. Woodcut, 1471.

Once, as a young man, I had arranged to spend the evening with a friend and to call for him at his room. On arrival, however, I found it empty, and a note on the table said:

I am ♡ccupied to-night

No further explanation was necessary. The figure of a heart in place of the "o" said everything. A heart—that is to say, a stylized representation of the human heart—is one of the most popular pictorial symbols of our time, connected with the view that the heart is the center of the human body and the seat of human emotions.

This importance was not attributed to the heart in ancient times. The feelings were centered in the liver or the stomach, it was thought (and anyone who has ever been afraid or in love will agree). Symbolical reproductions of a heart were rare. As a symbol the heart is chiefly a biblical and Christian phenomenon that became popular in the Middle Ages, first in religious art and ornamentation and later also in secular.

A heart stands first and foremost for every shade of earthly and celestial love: infatuation (often in this case pierced by an arrow), sexual love, neighborly love, human charity, love of God, and God's love for men. A heart is the attribute of a number of saints and can stand especially for the Virgin Mary and Jesus. There are countless examples of this, particularly in Roman Catholic churches. In 1765 the Catholic Church insti-

I am in love or we love each other. A heart, alone or pierced by Cupid's dart, is perhaps the best known and most widespread of all symbols. The trees, park benches, and school desks that have been carved with it, the fences and paving stones that it has been drawn on, can be counted by the million.

A heart with a cross on it occurs frequently in religious symbolism, here in the arms of Niels Steensen, or Nicolaus Steno (1638–86), a Roman Catholic bishop. Note, however, that this heart is not symmetrical but approximates in shape the anatomical heart. Steensen's scientific studies included the human heart.

tuted a special festival of the Sacred Heart of Jesus. Symbolically and metaphorically, a heart can stand for a great many other (sympathetic) feelings and characteristics: friendship, loyalty, sympathy, understanding, animation, vitality, human warmth, conviction, sincerity, honesty, self-sacrifice, piety, devotion, courage ("a manly heart"), goodness ("a kind heart"), and generosity. The oldest American war decoration, awarded to all "personnel killed or wounded in combat," is the Purple Heart, which is shaped like a heart.

In Denmark the heart has become increasingly a Christmas symbol, no doubt influenced by the woven paper heart made for hanging on the Christmas tree. In English-speaking countries the heart is especially associated with St. Valentine's Day, February 14, when heart-shaped presents are exchanged, and cards decorated with hearts are sent to persons of the opposite sex as "Valentines."

The Hand

Perhaps even more than the brain it is the hand that has enabled man to rise above the animals. It is with our hands that we have made and applied all our tools and implements, weapons, and other products from the time when our ancestors hurled the first missile at an opossum until, in 1978, we turn on or off our color-television set. It was also especially by means of their hands that some men raised themselves above other men. And it is largely with our hands that we indicate our feelings and intentions.

All this is reflected in language, spoken and written, and in the language of pictorial symbolism. We speak of "handicrafts," "handiness," "handiwork," "firsthand," "put in hand." And since antiquity the picture of a hand or two hands has carried the meaning of work, art, and craft, the work of men's hands.

The hand also stands for power, authority, mastery, possession. The emblem of the Roman legions was originally a hand. The Danish police badge is a hand enclosing an eye: an image anyone can understand. When Napoleon crowned himself emperor in 1804, he continued the tradition of the French kings and placed a hand at the tip of his imperial scepter. It was "the hand of justice" (*la main de justice*).

The hand has always played a big part in the judicial system, both as a symbol of the enforcement of justice (i.e., arrest and punishment of criminals) and as the raised hand of oath taking. In the latter form the hand often appears in court and county seals. The specimen pictured is from Sweden, 1571.

As a symbol of might or power the hand above all represents God, God's intervention in human life, God's blessing and salvation or God's punishment. The symbol was particularly prevalent in the first centuries of Christianity when there was a reluctance to show direct representations of God. A similar image is known in other religions. In Muslim countries a large hand is often seen painted at the entrance to a house. It is "the hand of Fatima," affording protection from evil, a prayer that God will "hold his hand over" the occupants of the house. And the power of God is transmitted through the hands of his servants when, by the laying on of hands, they consecrate, ordain, heal, and bless.

The flat, open hand says: "I conceal nothing, I am unarmed, I come in peace." Over most of the earth, to both men and gods, it is a sign of peace, friendship, trust; invocation, supplication, and worship. At the same time the clenched fist stands for hostility and attack or at any rate the threat of it. It is used by demonstrators and revolutionaries, communists and Black Panthers.

Renaissance book printer's mark. The printing works was owned by two brothers, and the hands denote the Latin motto *Bona fida* ("in good faith"— i.e., "with honest intentions, in full mutual honesty").

Perhaps the most universal employment of the hand or hands in symbolism is in the handshake. Even in ancient Rome this fine symbol indicated what two persons could "give their hand to": friendship and marriage and in an extended sense loyalty, a promise, an agreement, a contract, alliance, confirmation. The handclasp later became a common device on the banners of European trade unions, where it stood for fraternity and solidarity. Recently the ancient symbol has come to mean "development aid," the helping hand of rich countries to developing countries.

Outlined hands are common in French and Spanish cave paintings, usually in association with the animals desired by Stone Age man. Is this the oldest symbol of ownership in the world?

The Skull

At least it was easy to see which bottle in the medicine cupboard was the wrong one: the grinning death's head on the label said so plainly. Wherever it is vital to tell people to be extracareful, regardless of whether they can read the language (or can read at all)—with poison containers, with explosives, with high-tension cables—a skull conveys a warning that everyone can understand. It signifies "caution," "danger." In a related sphere, where one threatens or scares with the prospect of death, the message is conveyed by means of a skull (intensified perhaps by crossed bones). This is the case with the pirate flag and with certain military uniforms, such as the German Death's Head Hussars. The Nazi SS, with ghastly justification, wore a cap with a skull on it. But with what reason? Even though one should die—by drinking from the wrong bottle or at the hand of pirates—it is a long way from the dead body to the fleshless, bare skull. How many people have actually seen a skull?

In the art and symbolism of the Near East, Egypt, and classical Greece the human skull seems, generally speaking, to have been unknown. Similarly with the Roman Empire, and representations of skulls were rare in the early Middle Ages. As of the 14th century, however, the picture changes, and the skull becomes common in art. The reason was conceivably the frequency of major epidemics, especially the Black Death of the 1340s and 1350s, which wiped out a fourth of the population of Europe. Whole towns and districts were depopulated, leaving nobody to bury the dead. Skulls and skeletons were a daily sight, the proximity of death a day-to-day experience.

This experience, this certainty, caused people to react in one of two ways: either to always think of death and prepare themselves for the beyond or never to think of death but to enjoy themselves while they could! How these two reactions were apportioned among the living is hard to say, but in symbolism the former is all-pervasive. There *are* skulls that undoubtedly mean "Eat, drink and be merry," on drinking cups, for instance, but the great majority denote: "Remember that you have to die! Life is short, and death certain. Man is frail; all is vanity. Watch and pray!" A skull came to stand for the mortification of the flesh, for asceticism, remorse, penitence, renunciation of "this world." It was common in the coats of arms of the pious and threatened at one time to take over ecclesiastical ornamentation.

The fleshless grin, the empty sockets—you need not be able to read in order to understand the meaning of the label and to exercise care with the contents.

In a rather different connotation the skull came to stand for the life of the hermit and the anchorite, for meditation, philosophy, wisdom, the quest for the eternal verities, or the verities themselves—of time and eternity. Together with an ear of grain or some flowers a skull could signify the resurrection of the dead; with an apple or a serpent, the Fall; with a cross, Golgotha (which means "skull"). The skull became the attribute of a number of saints, especially those who had "bidden farewell to the world." In time it became an image of every sort of piety.

First and last, the skull remained a symbol of mortality and corruptibility, of the brevity of life and the "meaninglessness" of death. In this sense it recurs again and again in Renaissance and baroque ornamentation and pictorial art. The most famous literary example is the scene in which Hamlet apostrophizes the skull of Yorick: "Alas, poor Yorick! I knew him, Horatio, a fellow of infinite jest, of most excellent fancy: he hath bore me on his back a thousand times, and now how abhorred in my imagination it is! my gorge rises at it . . . where be your gibes now? your gambols, your songs, your flashes of merriment, that were wont to set the table on a roar? Not one now to mock your own grinning . . ." And that in a way is the message of all skulls: to be or not to be . . . ?

Cap badge of a British cavalry regiment. The traditional uniform of a hussar, with white cords across the chest and down the legs, is surely meant to suggest a skeleton. The squadron had to give the impression of being skeletons!

The Cap of Liberty

When a slave in ancient Rome was granted his freedom, the occasion was marked by the award of a cap for him to wear. A slave normally went bareheaded—only free men wore a headdress—and so a hat or cap became symbolic of civic liberty or freedom in general. When Brutus and his fellow conspirators murdered Caesar, whom they believed threatened the republican constitution, in 44 B.C., a commemorative coin was struck depicting a cap of liberty.

It was not only among the Romans that free people wore such a cap. It was common all around the Mediterranean and in the part of Asia Minor that was called Phrygia. The population, including fishermen, sailors, and pirates, were perhaps regarded as more freedom-loving than others; at any rate, the cap of liberty was often called the Phrygian cap.

In the late 18th century, with its romantic preoccupation with the ancient world, the Phrygian cap became a popular symbol of political liberty. When the United States rose against Britain in 1776, the Senate placed a cap of freedom in its seal, and a number of the states included one in their coats of arms.

Thirteen years later, in 1789, when the great revolution broke out in France, the Phrygian cap—now always red—became its central symbol. It probably began when liberated galley slaves arrived in Paris wearing red caps. The Jacobin Club, where the most extreme revolutionaries gathered, took the cap as its emblem, and on June 20, 1792 the mob, which had forced its way into the royal palace, made Louis XVI don the red cap of liberty.

The Jacobin cap (as it was often called) came to symbolize unrestricted liberty, republicanism, and representative government, the revolution's program of human rights, and its motto: Liberty, Equality, Fraternity. The cap vanished under Napoleon, but it was reintroduced later, chiefly as the headdress of the female figure "Marianne," personifying the French Republic. She is seen in full figure or as a bust in every public office in France, on coins and stamps, and in many other places.

From France the cap of liberty spread to Switzerland and Italy and to other countries. It became especially popular in Central and South America. When the populations there broke

When the French republic is personified, it is almost invariably as Marianne, a young, beautiful, enthusiastic, and idealistic woman, recognizable by her red cap of liberty. This is true of official representations and also to a large extent of unofficial ones, as, for example, in this political cartoon. Altogether symbols play an important role in the form of compressed information and comment in day-to-day political cartoons and sketches.

away from Spain at the beginning of the 19th century, a number of the new states placed the red cap in their national arms, among them Cuba, Haiti, Nicaragua, Salvador, Colombia, Bolivia, Paraguay, and Argentina. In Denmark the cap figured for many years in the symbolism of the Social Democrats.

It is also familiar to us in another way or rather two. It was not only the peoples of the Mediterranean who wore the cap. It was also worn farther north by Gauls and Teutons. In Scandinavia it became a part of the daily dress of peasants and fishermen and still is in the Faroe Islands. Finally, there is the pixie cap.

The gray knee breeches and coat and red cap of the pixie are what the peasantry wore in the distant past. How "free" that peasantry was is arguable, but at any rate the pixie is his own master and fully entitled to his red cap of liberty.

When Argentina gained its freedom from Spain in 1813, the new independent state placed the cap of freedom, held by the hands of brotherhood, in the middle of its national arms, with the whole enclosed by the wreath of victory and surmounted by a rising sun, symbol of a new dawn for the nation.

Tools and Weapons

A hammer is and was such an essential tool in almost every craft and occupation that it has come to stand for work, and, by extension, for the days when people work: that is, weekdays.

Above all the hammer is the smith's tool, and the smith has always felt himself to be in a class apart. Both on Olympus and in Scandinavian mythology there were gods who were also smiths: Hephaestos, Vulcan, Thor. And what of the steel and engineering workers' unions of today? Between these two extremes is the smiths' guild of the town of Ystad in Sweden, whose articles of association, dating from 1496, contain the following magnificent passage: "The guild of smiths is an office the world cannot dispense with. It is a support and help to every office. Without smiths no one can survive. As grammar is to other arts, indicating the way to other arts, so the art of the smith shows the way to the arts of the world. From smiths have come popes, cardinals, bishops, and leaders of the holy church; smiths have been emperors and kings."

A smith's hammer came to symbolize hard, honest work and indomitable strength. When the Communists came to power in Russia in 1917, they devised a new national emblem incorporating a sickle to symbolize farm workers and a hammer to symbolize industrial workers. Of the two the symbol of the hammer made the greatest appeal to people and nations, and it was copied by many other countries, not all of them communist. A hammer stood for the working class, for industry or the will to develop industry, and for the resolve to hammer at the existing society in order to reshape it. In the symbolism of freemasonry the hammer (probably a stone one) stands, inter alia, for determination.

But a hammer was not only a practical object. It was also magical. The smith, who kept company with iron and fire, was supposed to "know a thing or two" even in ancient times, as in the case of Wayland Smith. The Norse god Thor used his hammer for more than forging. When angry, he flung it, and then the lightning struck! When Christianity was introduced into Northern Europe in the 10th century, small reproductions of Thor's hammer were worn as charms by people who clung to the old faith. Many of these have been dug up in Scandinavia, and pictures of Thor's hammer are also known from runic stones. A hammer was a protecting and propitiating emblem, and that aspect of its function, perhaps, is what lives on in the

A fine example of a charm in the shape of Thor's hammer from the 10th century, found on the Baltic island of Bornholm. Usually of silver, such charms must have been produced in large numbers, as molds have been found that could make a whole series at a time. Some of the molds could be used both for Thor's hammer and for a cross, so the manufacturer could satisfy both newly converted Christians and adherents of the old faith!

The hammer and sickle of the Soviet Union. It was customary among leaders of the Russian Revolution to adopt symbolical names. "Hammer" in Russian is *molot*, and this word inspired the chairman of the Leningrad Soviet, Viateslav Skriabin, to take the name Molotov.

gavel of the parliamentary speaker and the auctioneer, whose "hammer blows" plainly indicate a decisive moment. There is a hammer in the emblems of several saints, among them Eligius, best known in English as St. Eloi, who was both a blacksmith and a goldsmith. And the word of God himself is a hammer, just as the prophet Jeremiah says: "Is not my word like as a fire? saith the Lord; and like a hammer that breaketh the rocks in pieces?"

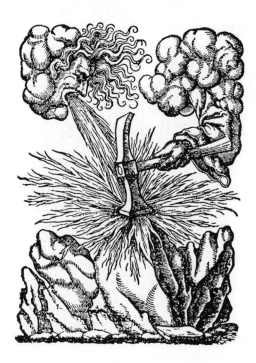

The word of the Lord, says Jeremiah, is like a hammer "that breaketh the rock in pieces." This mighty image appealed to users of words and was sometimes taken as the mark of book publishers.

The Scythe

The Greek god Kronos (Cronus) personified time. But he appears to have been originally the god of agriculture and harvesting: at any rate he is usually depicted holding a harvesting implement, a sickle. (That this could also be used for other things he demonstrated when he castrated his father, Uranus, with it.) In Roman mythology Saturn corresponded to Kronos. Among other things he was the god of agriculture and time, and, like Kronos, he was known by his sickle. When Renaissance man turned to classical antiquity, in a way resurrecting the Roman pantheon in art and history, technology had advanced beyond the classics. In Europe the sickle was no longer the only harvesting implement—there was also the scythe—and in pictorial representations Saturn was now more often identified by a scythe.

Saturn in his chariot, drawn by two dragons, with the signs of Capricorn and Aquarius as the wheels. Woodcut in *Poeticon Astronomicon*, Venice, 1485.

Time, Tempus, Father Time, with his scythe, here serrated. *Hanc aciem sola retundit virtus*—"This blade only virtue can resist"— he is saying. French printer's mark, 1546.

The scythe was also the attribute of a newly created allegorical figure, Tempus, or Time. The scythe symbolized time and the march of time. The pointer on a sundial was sometimes shaped like a scythe blade; the scythe seemed to be cutting out the hours of the day like slices of cake. Sometimes Tempus was represented as a young man but more commonly as an old (but not decrepit) one, as Father Time. Occasionally he would have diabolical features and frequently wings: "time flies," as we all know. He always had his scythe and often an hourglass (see a later chapter).

From the scythe as a symbol of "the march of time" it is not far to the idea of time's harvest. Just as the farmer's hay and wheat fall each year to his scythe, so we shall all one day succumb to the scythe of time, to death. The scythe became death's attribute. But often death was indistinguishable from time. Death, too, was an old man, perhaps winged, with a scythe and an hourglass. From the end of the 14th century, however, death was shown increasingly as a skeleton, as, for example, when he led the "Dance of Death." Skeleton and scythe were united, and everyone fell to the skeleton's scythe. The skeleton with a scythe became one of the most durable and widespread of European symbols, and our languages reflect it. We speak of the "Great Reaper," of "mowing down," and of Death's "harvest."

At the same time, however, the original meaning of the scythe lived on. The scythe could still stand for harvesting and for harvest in its real, direct sense, the crops of the field. A scythe is an attribute of summer as well as of hope. In almanacs it was the symbol of the month of July; in southern Europe, the month of the grain harvest; in northern Europe, the month of the hay harvest.

Medieval German woodcut showing Death flying over those who have fallen to his scythe. *Ego sum*—"I still exist"—he is saying.

The Axe

An axe is above all an implement for felling trees. It was the woodman's most important tool. But it must also be the instrument of the god of thunder. How else was the woodman to explain the trees, often the mightiest in the forest, that had been felled or split open by lightning in one colossal stroke? Lightning was the axe of the god of thunder. That was confirmed by the stone axes that were discovered in the ground. They were "thunder stones," the traces of old strokes of lightning.

This idea was current all over the Near East and Europe. The axe was an attribute of gods, especially gods of thunder, of lightning and of light. What we now call a thunderbolt was originally an axe, a throwing axe or perhaps a throwing hammer like that of the Norse god of thunder, Thor. In Mesopotamia the axe-bearing gods can be traced back to 3000 B.C. Later both Zeus, the thunderer of Greek mythology, and Apollo, the bringer of light, had an axe. Apollo was the patron of Troy, and the town had an axe on its coins. The axe was also identified with mighty gods in Crete and in the Bronze Age in Scandinavia. Often there were two gods together, each with an axe or perhaps with double axes. Processional axes, axes borne like an idol, are known both from Crete and from Scandinavian rock engravings. Possibly the axe itself was worshipped like a god.

At any rate axes, axe images, and models of axes were used as charms. In Scandinavia until quite recent times it was the practice to deposit an axe head under the foundations of a new house. If lightning was an axe, then, conversely, the axe might give protection against lightning.

The fact that the axe symbolized divine power, punishment, and retribution could, of course, only stimulate the use of the

Two Bronze Age gods wielding axes. Drawing made in 1779 of a metal figure, since lost, that was dug up in Denmark.

same symbol by earthly powers. The best-known example is that of the Roman fasces, a bundle of rods and an axe (a headsman's axe!) borne before the supreme authorities of the Roman Empire. It was naked power flaunting its methods of punishment: flogging and beheading. Fasces became the symbol of the civil authorities, of law enforcement and the judiciary. In many countries today they are a police emblem. During the 18th-century cult of ancient Rome fasces also became an image of the Roman republic and "the spirit of Rome." Representations of the bundle and axe were prominent during the French Revolution and were incorporated in contemporary republican symbolism in Europe and in North and South America. When Mussolini founded the Fascist movement in Italy in 1919, he took the fasces symbol as his party emblem and as an expression of both his objectives and his methods. The two words "fasces" and "Fascism" are of the same origin.

In 1940 Marshal Pétain chose a quite different axe, the old double axe of the Franks, the famous *franciska*, as the official emblem of the defeated French State, *l'Etat Français*, to replace the insignia of the Third Republic. It was shown on coins and stamps, among other things, probably to recall earlier and more glorious periods in the national history. But there may also have been another idea behind it: perhaps this axe was meant to avert evil and give protection from further "thunderbolts" on the part of the victorious Germans.

Finally, the axe is the attribute of a number of saints. In some cases it is the workman's axe: for example, that of the carpenter Joseph, the husband of Mary. In others it is the executioner's axe, the instrument of martyrdom, as in the case of the apostle Mathias. In other cases again it is the battleaxe, the most famous example of which is St. Olav of Norway, who was slain with an axe at the battle of Stiklestad on July 29, 1030. He became Norway's patron saint. The regalia of Norway in the Middle Ages comprised the crown, the scepter, the orb—and an axe. From ancient times Norway's arms had been a lion rampant, yellow on a field of red. In about 1280 an axe was placed in the lion's forepaws, and it is there to this day.

The Trident

As everyone knows, the trident belongs to Neptune, god of the sea. Neptune was Roman, and he took over the trident from the Greek Poseidon, likewise god of the sea but also a good deal more. He was the "earthshaker," splitting rocks and shattering mountains, dealing out thunder and lightning. Poseidon's three-pronged scepter may have originally represented stylized lightning or a thunderbolt, indicative of the force of lightning. Certain deities in Mesopotamian and Hittite mythology

Neptune, ruler of the waves, with his trident, drawn by dolphins. Xylograph, 18th century.

had a similar implement. If there is any connection, however, it had been forgotten in classical Greece. There Poseidon was chiefly the god of the sea, and the trident in particular indicated this and illustrated his dominion over the oceans.

Fish can be netted or hooked, but the biggest are usually caught or killed—if one can, for it takes skill, courage, and strength—with a spear, harpoon, or what is known as a fish spear, an implement that is indistinguishable from a trident. Tuna were caught in the Aegean with fish spears, and Poseidon was probably in origin an Aegean god. His trident indicated that he was master of the tuna and ruler over their realm, the sea.

The trident and Poseidon and the trident and Neptune were inseparable. And soon the trident itself became a symbol of the sea and everything belonging to it: navigation, trade and shipping, naval power and command of the sea. From antiquity until today it has appeared in countless numbers of maritime

After building his frontier wall between England and Scotland the Roman Emperor Hadrian (117–38) struck a coin for use in the province of Britannia showing the figure of a woman with a shield and lance—the spirit of Rome defending the province. In the 17th century the English used the figure again on a medal, later also on coins, but this time with the Union flag on the shield and a trident symbolizing naval power in place of the lance.

symbolical pictures and allegorical marine settings, in the ornamentation of warships, in the emblems of shipping companies, in the tattoos of sailors. In the personification of Britain as a shipping nation and naval power she was represented as Britannia, with helmet, shield, and trident. She held this high for several centuries, for example, on pennies. The picture was dropped in the currency reform of 1971.

It is not surprising that the trident was also associated with other marine divinities, such as Amphitrite, Neptune's wife, Nereus, the god of navigation; and his daughters, the Nereids. Or that it became the astronomical and astrological sign for the planet Neptune (discovered in 1846).

Strangely, however, the trident is also to some extent an attribute of Satan and the Devil and, from the 14th century, probably by derivation, of Death. The explanation may be the death-dealing instrument's appearance. With its three barbed prongs it looks malignant. It is a plausible elaboration of Satan's poker or the Devil's spit. But there may also be an historical explanation. A certain class of gladiators in ancient Rome were armed with a trident (and a net, indicating yet again that the trident at that time was regarded as a fishing implement). During persecutions of the Christians many of them were doubtless killed in Roman amphitheaters by such trident-wielding executioners. Several of the first Christian saints have a trident as their attribute, commemorating their martyrdom in the arena. Could it be that this use of the trident in the hands of enemies of Christianity made it a symbol among Christians of the Antichrist himself?

The Knife

The knife is one of the most basic implements, almost universal in use. To the hunter and fisher it is indispensable: for
killing and skinning game, gutting fish, and cutting a stick. It
is equally so to the artisan, whether carver or tanner, saddler,
furrier, or shoemaker. The gardener uses a knife for grafting,
pruning, or tying. The housewife uses knives in the kitchen and
on the table. The butcher uses knives, as do the surgeon and
the barber; likewise, the monk and the scribe, for cutting
parchment and making quills. The headsman uses knives, as
does the killer, both the murderer and the patriot who rids his
country of a tyrant. Priests use knives for killing the animal to
be sacrificed.

There is no end to the number of people who use knives, and
more or less corresponding to many of these practical uses are
symbolical ones. A table knife (and fork) used in timetables

"She is long-haired in front but smooth at the back," so it is not easy to catch
the favorable moment as she flies past on winged feet. She is easily identifiable
here by her coiffure and her knife. Woodcut from the 16th century.

The apostle Bartholomew with the gospels and, notably, the knife for which he is known. Wood-carving on house, c. 1515, Naestved, Denmark.

and tourist literature denotes a restaurant or cafeteria. The penknife of the scribe is an attribute of Grammatica, the mythological female figure representing linguistic studies and the art of writing. The assassin's dagger, symbolizing hatred and vengeance, is the attribute of Invidia, or Envy, one of the seven deadly sins, who sometimes conceals it in her sleeve. The weapon of murder can also, however, symbolize the murdered one, as, for instance, the Dominican saint Peter the Martyr, who is shown with a knife embedded in his breast or head or both. A cheese knife is an attribute of St. Lucius; a razor, of Occasio, the propitious moment, the occasion to be seized, like a clean-shaven man held firmly by his single lock of hair. An executioner's knife is the stock symbol of the apostle Bartholomew, who was flayed alive. Sometimes he is shown with the knife in one hand and his flayed skin in the other. His day is August 24, St. Bartholomew's Day, the calendar sign of which is a knife. Bartholomew is the patron saint of all knife users but especially of workers in hides and leather.

In Christian art, however, the knife is chiefly associated with Abraham in two or three different senses. As narrated in chapter 22 of Genesis, God wanted to put Abraham to a test: he was commanded to sacrifice his son Isaac to God. Obeying the command, Abraham "stretched forth his hand, and took the knife to slay his son." The gruesome scene of Abraham holding the knife and Isaac the fuel for his own sacrifice has been interpreted as a prefiguration, a symbolical parallel to Jesus carrying his own cross to Golgotha, there to be "sacrificed" for the sake of mankind. The sacrificial knife in Abraham's hand points forward to the "sacrificial death" of Jesus.

But Abraham with his knife can also symbolize something quite different. Abraham is preeminent among patriarchs. His yielding to God's will, even when it must have seemed to him utterly inhuman, makes him the most typical example of Old Testament fear of and submission to God. At the same time, his knife, the sacrificial knife, symbolizes the animal sacrifices —and, in his case, almost human sacrifices—that were characteristic of Jewish religious practices that Christianity repudiated. Abraham with his knife could therefore symbolize Synagoga, the personification in Christian art of Jewry as something objectionable.

Because of his hospitable reception of the three men on the plains of Mamre Abraham is also the patron saint of hoteliers and innkeepers. In former times the patriarch, recognizable by his large sacrificial knife, was a common feature on inn signs.

Compasses

To the ancient thinkers and technicians geometry was not only a science of immense practical value—in surveying and partitioning areas of land and in all types of construction—but was also, with its irrefutably true propositions and captivatingly clear proofs, something more, something "higher," almost something divine. This view was adopted by the scholastics of the Middle Ages. Geometry was sublime. Its methods— measuring, calculating, and inference—and its indisputable results made it a model. And its most important instrument, a pair of compasses, became the attribute and symbol of a number of ideal characteristics.

They included Prudentia, prudence, discernment, human knowledge; Temperantia, temperance, moderation, self-control; Justitia, justice, impartiality, fairness; Veritas, truth, veracity, incorruptibility. All were characteristics to be desired in a ruler, and compasses became a symbol of the good, wise, just king. Later, under the absolute rulers, compasses came to denote something different. The two legs symbolized the monarch as both the center of the state and the regulator of the life and activity of his subjects.

A pair of compasses, of course, could also represent the persons and occupations that actually used them, especially architects and builders but also, for example, geographers and astronomers, together with their allegorical counterparts: Architecture, Geometry (one of the seven liberal arts), Urania, the muse of astronomy, and so on. From the architects the

The symbolical properties of compasses must have appealed particularly to printers. They occur again and again in printers' marks. This one is Spanish, from 1566.

freemasons took over the compasses as a symbol, usually combined with another mason's tool, the square.

The symbol of the compasses was also associated with the greatest architect of all, namely, the Creator of the universe. When God was represented in his capacity of Creator of the World, Deus Artifex, he was invariably shown holding a pair of compasses. Perhaps there was some extra symbolism in the similarity of the compass legs to a large A, alpha, the first letter of the alphabet, signifying the beginning of all things.

Saturn in Roman mythology was also given a pair of compasses as an attribute. He was originally the god of agriculture. From this in turn derived the surveying and division of agricultural land, denoted by the compasses. It can sometimes be hard to tell whether the picture of an old man with a pair of compasses (plus, perhaps, regalia and a book) represents the Lord God or Saturn. As Saturn was also the god of melancholy, his compasses became one of the attributes of Melancholy.

Along with Aldus' anchor and dolphin the most famous printer's mark from earlier times is surely the pair of compasses, held from above, that Christopher Plantin used when he founded a printing press at Antwerp, called De gulden Passer, in 1558. In the following centuries his successors varied the mark in countless ways.

In the symbolical art of the Renaissance compasses also stood for intellect and genius, in time particularly for the combination of intellectual and physical creativity. One leg of the compasses stood still in the middle; the other made the long journey round the perimeter. Compasses came to symbolize all creative work that combined the theoretical with the physical, standing for "brain and hand," and in turn for unity and cohesion. A characteristic example of compasses used in this sense is the trademark of the famous printing dynasty of Plantin in Antwerp. The compasses are held by the hand of God, and the *Labore et Constantia* ("Work and Constancy") of the motto elaborates the picture: one leg symbolizes diligent physical activity, the other the firm intellectual standpoint.

And the compass symbol lives on! When East Germany wanted national arms after the Second World War, a hammer was chosen, following the example of the Soviet Union. In 1953, however, this was changed to a hammer and a pair of compasses, the latter symbolizing "technical intelligence." In other words, the hammer represents manual workers, the compasses intellectual workers. In 1959 this emblem was also incorporated in the East German national flag. And when Italy instituted an international prize for aesthetically outstanding industrial art and design in 1954, it was named *Compasso d'Oro*, or Golden Compasses.

The Arrow

Until the invention of gunpowder and bullets—that is to say, during by far the greater part of human history—an arrow shot from a bow was the fastest phenomenon known to man. Furthermore, the arrow had an important quality that was lacking in gunpowder: it was noiseless. An arrow became an image for speed, swiftness, haste, and zeal. It also symbolized unexpectedness, being taken by surprise.

Of all things that can take anyone by surprise, the most popular, undoubtedly, is love, and an arrow came above all to symbolize love and suddenly falling in love. Both Greeks and Romans invariably furnished the gods of love, Eros, Amor, and Cupid, with a bow and arrow or simply with an arrow. Expressions such as "Cupid's arrows,' or "love's arrows" have gone

Cupid, the god of love. He comes as swiftly as the dart that he holds in his hand, and that is his identification mark. And he is stronger than a lion. In this relief from 1828 by the Danish sculptor Bertel Thorvaldsen, however, the lion represents more specifically the "element" that is the earth. The picture is one of a series on Cupid's sovereignty over the four elements—i.e., about the omnipotence of love.

into every western language. And it has made no difference to the vitality of the symbol that bows and arrows have long since gone out of use and that most people have never seen an arrow being shot. One does not have to go far where young people are found before coming across a drawing with the bittersweet evidence of a heart pierced by an arrow.

An altogether different sudden guest is death. It comes when you least expect it. In the Middle Ages an arrow became the symbol of sudden, unexpected death and of the surprising and inexplicable illnesses with which it "struck" men and women. Death was shown as an old man or a skeleton holding an arrow. Epidemics and premature death were regarded as punishments from above, and so an arrow could also stand for the wrath of God. In the rebus symbols of the Renaissance an arrow sometimes means "the inevitable" (which, according to circumstances, could be virtually anything).

In ancient Rome an arrow together with a fish illustrated the paradoxical maxim *festina lente* (make haste slowly). The fish stood for slowness, because it was thought to impede ships. And in present-day Denmark two arrows are included with the postillion's horn in the emblem of the Postal and Telegraph Service. They stand for the telegraph service: quick, noiseless, and sometimes extremely surprising.

The Staff

A boy who is out walking in, say, a wood or in an unfamiliar part of his home town will almost invariably at the first opportunity find himself a stick, a switch, or a cudgel to walk with. Stick in hand, he is master of the situation. He can poke or flick and make his presence felt by animals and juniors. And, if need be, he can hit out with the stick and keep unwanted persons at their distance. But the mere fact of having a stick in his hand is an insurance against disagreeable incidents. When anybody can see the stick and know that it can be used, there will normally be no necessity to use it. That is the secret of the stick. "Speak softly and carry a big stick—you will go far," said Theodore Roosevelt.

From the earliest times the stick or staff has been the manifestation of power. The staff can be used to strike, castigate, or punish. It is longer than an arm and strikes harder than a hand. Its elementary message is: "Do what I say or you'll be beaten!" The staff became a symbol of power, authority, absolute might, sovereignty, or, seen from the other side, obedience. Under its Greek name *skeptron* ("scepter"), the staff became a symbol of rule, an attribute of kings and emperors; together with the crown, the most important outward manifestation of their rule.

Other persons entitled to claim obedience also had a staff as the sign of this right and the power behind it: judges, bishops, and masters of a guild had their staffs, and in many a European village the constable carried one as the outward sign of his authority. If a man abused his authority and was deprived of it, he also lost his staff. If this occurred legally by sentence of court, the staff was broken. In Christian art Synagoga, representing Jewry, was often depicted as a woman blindfolded (she refused to see the truth) and holding a broken staff.

The holder of power need not personally carry the staff, provided that it is there and can be seen. According to a Danish law of 1522, when a town recorder moved about the town on official business, a hazel stick had to be borne before him. The small procession with the stick bearer at its head is a humble echo of the Roman lictors, officials, sometimes a whole procession of them, who on ceremonial occasions bore bundles

A person in authority with some of his subordinates. His long staff and his assistant's short one indicate their authority and right to command. Detail of a Dutch tapestry, c. 1470. (Museum of Applied Art, Copenhagen)

of faggots (fasces) and an axe before the high officials of the Republic and the Empire. The Roman faggots and axe became a general symbol of executive authority and are still used today, by judicial and police authorities, for example, in many countries. Or they have simply become a symbol of state authority, particularly in republics. Thus the fasces are included in the national arms of, among other countries, Cuba, Ecuador, and Bolivia.

In Britain the Speaker of the House of Commons has a staff of office that commands immense respect. This is the mace, which lies in front of him, visible to all, at every session of Parliament. The mace is regarded almost as much as a symbol of parliamentary authority in general, however, and the legislative assemblies of other Commonwealth countries have all produced a mace as a manifestation of their authority. When the Bahama Islands became independent in 1973, they included a representation of their mace in the Prime Minister's flag. British local governments can also have a mace, symbolizing local rule, and there is a similar institution in Switzerland. In former times, at least, universities would have their scepter, borne publicly on ceremonial occasions as a demonstration of the university's independence and right to govern its own affairs.

In visual art the staff became an attribute both of the supreme gods, Jupiter and Juno, for example, and of personifications of forces or qualities that are sovereign—Fate or Vanity—or that should be sovereign, such as Virtue and Truth.

Even the mightiest of rulers, however, cannot be in more than one place at a time. He has to exercise his authority through deputies—representatives, ambassadors, and heralds. In order that they may meet with respect, they will often bear a staff. Since ancient times a staff or stick has been the herald's or messenger's symbol—and protection. By marking the person out as an emissary it was also meant to guarantee him against molestation, which would be particularly important in case of negotiators between belligerents. The staff made them "inviolate."

The messengers of God, the archangels, are also known by their staff: Gabriel, who made the annunciation to Mary, as well as Raphael and Michael. And Hermes, the Greek Mercury, the messenger of Zeus, carried his famous caduceus, originally just a branch but in time a wand furnished with wings and with two serpents twined about it. Like negotiators between men, Mercury was a mediator, a peacemaker, and so his winged caduceus came to stand for conciliation, toleration, peace, and the blessings of peace: commerce and prosperity.

Ambassadors and heralds may also have had their staffs in order to thump the floor and get a hearing when they had to proclaim and announce. The same explanation no doubt applies to the staffs of the master of ceremonies and lord chamberlain. Regardless of any practical applications, however, it was still the staff's symbolical value that was the essential factor. Two of the highest British offices of state and the court are called simply by the staff of their office and its color, namely Black Rod and White Rod.

An especially famous staff is the marshal's baton, the symbol of the field marshal's rank and authority. Its symbolism was so strong that the marshal's name and titles receded and he was quite simply the "staff," the headquarters from which his orders issued. From this we get "staff service" and "general staff." The marshal's baton also had practical application. It is easier to point and indicate with a staff in one's hand. With tens of thousands of soldiers scattered over a wide area, orders and commands can be made much plainer with the aid of a staff. The swagger stick of British officers resembles the field marshal's baton in this respect. It may even be used for prodding and urging on or for striking, as Frederick the Great of Prussia used to belabor his grenadiers when he thought they were not attacking hard enough.

In this respect the field marshal's baton is akin both to the schoolmaster's pointer and the conductor's baton. And from the latter, in turn, perhaps via the drum major, there is a link with the staff that in ancient Greece distinguished professional reciters and minstrels, the "rhapsodists." In order to keep the correct time and rhythm when reciting or singing, they marked the time with their staff.

Whoever gets strength from God can do things that otherwise only God can do. We have God's own words for this in Exodus: "And thou shalt smite the rock, and there shall come

The staff has power over the elements, and with his rod Moses struck water from the rock. It also has power over nature, and with her magic staff the sorceress Circe turned Odysseus's men into pigs. Here Circe is shown with her wand on a Greek vase.

water out of it," the Lord said to Moses. As for the instrument of God's strength, could that be anything but the staff? "And Moses lifted up his hand, and with his rod he smote the rock twice: and the water came out abundantly."

In the right hands the staff has power over the elements as well as over health and sickness. Whoever Bacchus struck with his staff would fall into ecstasies. The sorceress Circe turned Odysseus's men into swine with a stroke of her staff. It is in the language: we are "smitten with madness." The staff can also drive out spirits and restore health. Aesculapius, the god of medicine and of healing, had his staff, and the caduceus of Hermes caused men to fall into the sweetest of sleeps.

Another wonderful staff was Aaron's rod, as told in the book of Numbers. When God wanted to appoint Israel's first high priest, he said: ". . . the man's rod, whom I shall choose, shall blossom." The next morning Aaron's rod had "brought forth buds, and bloomed blossoms, and yielded almonds." To Christianity this miracle of growth, the dried stick that blossomed, came to symbolize both the virgin birth and the chosen of God. Kings of Europe put a lily on their scepter in order to show that their staff "had blossomed" and that they were God's chosen. To Freud, the rod itself and the fresh buds that it grew were a phallic symbol and an image of male fertility. One of D. H. Lawrence's books about sexual emancipation is entitled *Aaron's Rod*.

Priests had staffs, whatever their religion: prophets, readers of omens, augurs, oracles, soothsayers, and miracle men. Magicians and conjurers indeed have theirs: the rods of Moses and Aaron became a conjurer's wand. It was not a far cry from one to the other. The magic formula "Hocus pocus" spoken by the conjurer as he waves his wand is only a garbled version of the Latin words *Hoc est corpus* ("This is the body") from the consecration of the bread and wine in the Catholic mass.

Before choosing Aaron's rod as the one to blossom God did not ask whether everyone had a rod or staff; as they were wandering in the desert they all did. Besides other uses, the staff is also the wanderer's commonest and most necessary companion. A staff symbolizes wandering and journeying on foot, especially on pilgrimages; it is therefore the attribute of the patron saints of pilgrims, particularly St. James and St. Bridget

In the Middle Ages the kings of Europe began to put a lily flower on their scepters; it was their "Aaron's rod," budding and flowering. The lily scepter symbolized the fact that they had been chosen by God, that they were "by grace of God king." Picture of the three wise men with King Herod in a 12th-century psalter. (Royal Library, Copenhagen)

of Sweden. A special group of wanderers are the beggars, and the staff can also stand for beggary, poverty, abjectness, and powerlessness. In Danish it is said of one who has lost all his possessions and been reduced to beggary that he has been "brought to the beggar's staff."

Having to walk with a stick may also be a consequence of growing old. The riddle asked by the Sphinx was: "What goes on four feet, on two feet, and finally on three?" The answer given by Oedipus was: "Man. First he crawls on all fours, then he walks erect, and in old age he supports himself with a staff." Consequently, frailty and old age can also be symbolized by the staff, although this is practically the opposite of what it chiefly stands for: power and authority. What look like opposites can, however, be combined.

Authority is not based only on the ability to strike and inflict pain. It is also founded on experience, wisdom, knowledge of human nature, discernment, the ability to give shrewd advice and make the right decisions. All these are qualities normally found more frequently in the old (and weak) than among the young (and strong). In every language words meaning "old" or "elderly" have at the same time expressed veneration and respect. For instance, the Latin *senior*, which means "older," has become in French *seigneur* ("Your Highness" or simply "Lord God"), in French and English *Sire* ("Your Majesty"), and in English both the respectful address "sir" and the British title of nobility "Sir." The staff as a symbol of authority stands both for threats and punishment, the crude power of authority, and for the authority that is founded on the experience and wise decisions of age.

In the latter sense, at any rate, the fathers of the Christian church could use the staff. Bishops, abbots, and other princes of the church all had their staffs, often terminating in a cross, but the church symbolism was reinforced further in a rather different form of staff than we have so far considered, namely the crook or crosier. A shepherd's first duty is to keep his flock together. This he does, among other things, by means of his long shepherd's crook, one end of which is shaped like a hook. Should a sheep or a lamb break away from the flock, he can quickly catch it by hooking its leg or its neck with his crook. In ancient civilizations in which wealth, status, and power

A 14th-century tombstone in Tyrsted Church, Denmark. The inscription gives only the man's name, but the picture shows that he had been a pilgrim, indicated both by his staff and by the scallop shell on his bag. The palm branch may indicate that he had visited Jerusalem.

rested on animal stocks, the shepherd's crook came to symbolize just these and so became an attribute of rulers. Thus the Egyptian pharaohs had a stylized shepherd's crook as one of the emblems of their royal dignity.

Jesus calls himself "the good shepherd." The image of the shepherd and his flock, that is to say, the priest or clergyman and his congregation, entered in countless ways into the Church's gospel and propaganda. The Lutheran clergyman is styled "Pastor," which is Latin for "shepherd." An official proclamation by a bishop is called a "pastoral letter." It is no wonder, therefore, that the Church also adopted the shepherd's crook. In the course of time its hook developed into a curved head, but the shepherd symbolism is still present, the crosier being therefore at least doubly symbolical besides having a doubtless practical function as a support while standing during hour-long services (seats in churches are relatively recent).

It is characteristic of the staff that it often combines several different functions and several different sorts of symbolism. The schoolmaster's cane is both a pointer and an instrument of punishment (and an attribute of Grammatica, a name that could be translated as "the art of cramming"). The policeman's truncheon can be used for directing the traffic or for striking. The staff of the archangel Raphael marks him out as the emissary of God and also as the fellow traveler of Tobias and patron saint of all foot travelers. The rod of Moses is the chieftain's staff, a wanderer's staff, and a magic wand. Harlequin's wand can be used both for striking and for conjuring. The staff encompasses almost every symbolism, from the most exalted power to the most abject impotence; from Napoleon with his golden coronation staff to the beggar with his crutch by the wayside.

Household Objects

The Key

Whoever holds the key can open and close. He can let himself in; he can let others in; he can keep people out; and he can lock them up. To hold the key to something is to have control over it, and that is what the key came to symbolize: control, power, mastery.

"He," we have said, but perhaps "she" would have been more correct. The original "power of the keys"—the point of departure for all other key symbolism—in fact belongs outstandingly to the world of women. A key denotes the person in charge of the house, with its stores and reserves; that is to say, the housewife, the mistress of the house. The wedding ceremony of ancient Rome included the presentation of a key to the bride. The biblical Martha, "cumbered about much serving," is often depicted in art with a bunch of keys. She is the patron saint of housewives. In monasteries and nunneries a ring of keys was the insignia of the brother or sister who had charge of stores and housekeeping. Control of the house keys in Germanic law was the first claim to legal marriage, and, if a

167

housemaid had such "key control" (*Schlüsselgewalt*) for three years, she was automatically equal by law to the husband's rightful wife. The key represented wifely virtues, good house-keeping and administration, authority, responsibility, "office." From there it was not far to discretion, the ability to keep a secret and a confidence. At the Danish and Swedish courts a key is the badge of rank of a chamberlain, hung discreetly at the back of his uniform.

It was not only a house, a chest, or the royal cabinet that could be locked or unlocked. The city gates could be, and to the citizens the "keys of the city" symbolized their right to govern their own affairs. When the city received official guests whom it particularly wanted to honor, they might be presented with the keys of the city. The practice is still kept up. Conversely, when a city or a fortress had to surrender to a besieger, the occasion was marked by presenting the successful assail-

St. Peter in a medieval English stone carving. His attribute, the key of heaven, was interpreted quite literally as a gate key, an interpretation that has given rise to innumerable pious (and not so pious) stories about St. Peter as the guardian of the gates of heaven.

Bulla contra Erro
res Martini Lutheri et sequacium.

Keys as papal arms appear here in the coat of arms of Pope Leo X (a Medici). It is scarcely an accident that they look menacing. The woodcut is on the papal bull condemning the errors of Martin Luther and his fellow partisans of 1520.

ant with the keys of the city, as can be seen in the famous painting by Velazquez in 1635 of the surrender of Breda, *Las Lanzas*. The city itself could indeed be a key if it occupied a "key position." Such cities, usually fortress towns, sometimes have a key in their coat of arms. They include Gibraltar, the key to the Mediterranean.

All the symbolic keys of the world are, however, but trifles compared with the key—or the two keys—that have dominated the symbolism of keys—the keys of heaven. "And I say also unto thee, that thou art Peter, and upon this rock I will build my church; and the gates of hell shall not prevail against it. And I will give unto thee the keys of the kingdom of heaven: and whatsoever thou shalt bind on earth shall be bound in heaven: and whatsoever thou shalt loose on earth shall be loosed in heaven." So, according to the gospel of St. Matthew, spoke Jesus to the apostle Peter. From Peter in turn the bishops of

Rome, that is, the popes, received their power to "bind" and "loose," and the quoted passage is therefore one of the most significant to the Catholic Church.

It is easy to see why the key became the attribute of St. Peter. It occurred in ancient times and is the oldest individual attribute of a saint known to us. But the key was not merely that of the dead apostle: it also belonged to any living successor to the "throne of St. Peter" who had inherited his power to admit (to eternal bliss) or exclude (in everlasting perdition). As the papal emblem two crossed keys were nearly always used; known from the 13th century, the two keys developed during succeeding centuries into the coat of arms of the Papacy and the Catholic Church. They are used today as the state arms of the Vatican and of innumerable former and present church offices and possessions.

An example is the town of Naestved in Denmark, which grew up around a monastery and was originally owned by the Church. From the 13th century the keys were included in the town's seal and arms but were removed at the Reformation.

The key stood for power: spiritual, worldly, even purely physical power. In a 1567 woodcut illustrating Revelation Virgilio Solis shows the angel overcoming the serpent by driving it into the abyss with a giant key.

The keys signified not least the sale of indulgences; more than anything else they were an image of "papism," and the Protestants hated them. Their place in the town's arms was taken by a crown. By about 1900, however, tempers had sufficiently cooled for the town to be able to resume its old emblem, and its arms today display both the keys and the crown.

There were other variations of the celestial keys. A long succession of minor saints copied St. Peter, and cities that were dedicated to him or other such saints would often add keys to their arms, including Geneva, Bremen, Ostend, Riga, and many more. A key became the attribute of Ecclesia, the Church, and of Fides, the Faith. Charms for the pious were shaped like a key. Naturally enough, a key was also the emblem of the gatekeeper's guild (St. Peter being the gatekeeper of Heaven), of the locksmiths' guild (whose patron saint was St. Peter), and of prison warders, watchmen, and treasurers as well as, more recently, of hotel porters.

The Hourglass

That a measuring instrument should lead to thoughts of what is measured is nothing extraordinary. A pair of scales leads one to think of weighing, and a thermometer creates associations connected with temperature. So, too, with the measuring device we call an hourglass. It illustrates time and in art is the emblem of the gods who personify Time, the Greek Kronos and the Roman Saturn. Not, however, before the Middle Ages. The "sandglass" does not seem to have been invented until the 8th century, and, for good reasons, therefore, the classical world was prevented from giving its time gods the hourglass as an attribute.

From "time" it was only a step to the "passage of time," time slipping ceaselessly away (as the sand drops without pause from the upper globe of the hourglass), the relentless march of the years. From the Renaissance the hourglass in this sense was sometimes shown winged: a symbol that was particularly popular in the 18th century. And from "time flying," the allotted span of years inexorably running out, there was only another step to Death. By the 14th century, especially after the great plague epidemics in the middle of the century, a human skeleton had become a common image of Death, and the skeleton would usually be holding an hourglass. The hourglass had become the attribute of Death, usually combined from the Renaissance with a scythe (see a previous chapter). In the private sign language of priests, used in parish registers, there are examples of the picture of an hourglass indicating "burial."

Used alone, the hourglass became especially a symbol of the certainty of death and the brevity of life. It was a memento mori that said: "Remember you will die!" To some people this was a call to grasp the moment and enjoy life. To others it was the signal for sorrow, melancholy, and gloom. The hourglass came to symbolize Melancholy; it stood for the irrevocably lost, for the wretchedness of earthly life, the corruptibility of the body, the futility of all things, and of "vanity," in Latin *vanitas*.

In more subtle symbolical constructions the hourglass could stand for youth or age, depending on how much sand there was left in the top glass. The actual process of measur-

The skeleton shows the mercenary that his time is up. Woodcut by Albrecht Dürer, 1510.

ing, the unhurried pace of the hourglass's function, made it a symbol of Temperantia, of temperance and moderation. Finally, the hourglass could symbolize Truth, "time's daughter" (when all the sand has run out, it will be seen whether anything was hidden), and, by extension again, History.

The hourglass can also symbolize Eternity, and this once gave me an idea. In mathematics there is a sign rather like a figure eight lying on its side—∞—which means "infinite." In a flash I saw that this sign was an hourglass laid down: the sand could no longer run; time had stood still. Could Eternity and Infinity be better illustrated? It was a subtle idea. And a wrong one. There is no connection between the hourglass and the mathematical sign for infinity. In the world of symbols one has to tread warily.

The Chair

To sit in an elevated position when others are sitting on the ground or the floor or, perhaps even better, to sit down when others are standing indicates (in the true sense of the word) a place apart. The person who is seated has more dignity than the one who stands; he has a social and therefore a psychological superiority; his seated position expresses rank, authority, the right to command. This is connected with the fact that it is more comfortable to sit than to stand. Greater comfort—the standing person thinks—is due to the higher ranking, older, wiser, and more experienced. And to the seated person himself it is almost impossible not to make the commonest mistake in the world, to think that, because he is better off than others, he is also better than others.

Since ancient times the chair, the seat, has been a sign of the ruler and an attribute of gods. Probably the earliest surviving specimens are the folding chairs, identical in construction with modern folding stools, that are known from Egyptian royal tombs of about 1400 B.C. Similar chairs have been found in the graves of Danish chieftains of the Bronze Age c. 1000 B.C.

Another form of folding chair, rather heavier but still without back and armrest, was used in republican Rome and later by the highest officers of state, supreme judges and senators. It was a piece of furniture, but in addition it was in the highest degree a symbol of the authority, power, and dignity of the office concerned. It was called a *sella curulis*, or "carriage chair," because it was originally used on the official carriages of the supreme magistracy. The right to a *sella curulis* could be granted, among others, to victorious generals, and Caesar was awarded one in ivory by the Senate. How great this honor was is indicated by the fact that a coin bearing the chair was struck.

A quite different type of a ruler's seat may be just as old as the folding chair. This is the "throne," usually formed as a solid chair, with back and arms, as "majestical" as possible. The throne was the seat of rulers, kings, and emperors. On medieval seals the king was nearly always shown seated on his throne; that was how he was ideally supposed to exercise his functions, and the word "throne" became identified with the king, royalty, and monarchy just as much as "crown." We speak of the "heir and the successor to the throne," of the "speech from the throne," "abdication of the throne." The throne stood for power, rule, dignity, wisdom, and justice.

Biblical descriptions of life in heaven in the presence of God often reflect ancient court ceremony, and the Bible is full of references to the throne of God. In Revelation alone it is mentioned 38 times. "The Lord's throne is in heaven," we read in the Book of Psalms, but in art God is usually represented seated on a "normal" throne, symbolic of his sublimity, omnipotence, and glory. At ancient synods there would be an empty throne bearing a copy of the gospels or a wreath. It meant the unseen presence of God. There was something like this in the period of royal absolutism in Denmark, where a throne always stood in the Supreme Court, not only *for* the king (and of

The people sit on the ground while King Solomon sits comfortably aloft on his throne, a blanket behind him and a cushion under his feet. Medieval book miniature.

course usually empty) but in a certain sense also *equal to* the king. When the Virgin Mary was declared "divine" at the synod of Ephesus in 431, permission was given to depict her seated on a throne.

As the Christian church grew in strength and its leaders, the bishops, marked themselves out as persons of importance, they adopted to some extent both the folding chair and the throne as symbols of their office and dignity. This was especially the case after the Emperor Constantine in the 4th century had recognized the Church and granted its bishops judicial powers in civil cases and thus official legal authority.

Already in the 2nd century, however, the Church had taken over a third form of chair that was to prove of much greater significance. This was the "teacher's chair," in Greek the *cathedra*, which was sometimes shaped like a reading desk, something like a rostrum. Both inside and outside the church this seat of episcopal office and authority came to have enormous symbolic significance. The particular church where the bishop's *cathedra* was kept (that is to say, displayed on an elevation) was named after it. It was the "church of the chair," in Latin *ecclesia cathedralis*, from which we get our "cathedral." The Bishop of Rome, that is, the Pope, and the papal government were called the Holy See, from the Latin for "seat" (*sedem*). And when the Pope speaks *ex cathedra* ("from the chair"), he is infallible—no less.

From the bishop's *cathedra* and the dogma issuing from it the word came to stand for indisputable authority and doctrinaire opinion. In some countries the word in variant forms came to mean the schoolmaster's desk. In Denmark as late as the 1930s for a schoolchild to be called up to the *kateder* meant to be dragged over the coals. It was to be called to account

On the left the teacher at his desk with other insignia of authority, book, candlestick, and cane. The pupils are sitting on the floor. On the right the head of the family in his chair, with children and servants kneeling before him. Woodcut by Olaus Magnus, 1555.

before the throne of authority, usually to be corrected or punished.

A fourth form of symbolical seating accommodation that we may include is the stool. In the 16th century the French king as a special mark of favor introduced the custom of allowing dukes and a few other high-ranking persons to be seated in his own and the queen's presence. Not, of course, on a comfortable chair like themselves but on a stool. To "have a stool" became a highly valued privilege. Dowager duchesses kept their husbands' "stool right," but if they remarried (to someone of lower rank), they lost the right. More than one duchess is said to have declined the offer of an attractive marriage so as not to forgo her stool: that is to say, the rank and honor it symbolized. In the 18th century members of the council of state and ministers were also granted "stools," that is, the right to be seated in the king's presence, and the word "stool" became synonymous with "ministerial office." In Danish, the term is often employed in a slightly malicious sense, as, for instance, in phrases like "sticking to his stool"—clinging at all costs to office.

A Danish politician tempting a colleague with a ministerial appointment, symbolized by the stool, originally the one that the king of France allowed his ministers to sit on when in his presence. Cartoon by Poul Erik Poulsen, 1975.

The Ladder

We cannot all be equally well up in our Bible, but even those of us who have forgotten most of what we learnt as children remember the story of Jacob's ladder. Of how Jacob, the son of Isaac, spending the night at a holy place when going abroad, dreams of a ladder "set up on the earth, and the top of it reached to heaven: and behold the angels of God ascending and descending on it. And, behold, the Lord stood above it. ...."

Jacob's ladder: it was the way between earth and heaven, between man and God. If you are at all familiar with what we call a ladder, the image follows almost of itself, and indeed it was a widespread symbolic theme in the ancient oriental and classical world. In Egyptian, Jewish, and Greek sepulchral art, the "soul's ladder" is an image of spiritual and religious aspiration, of the human soul striving "for the heights." The ladder is also mentioned in this connection in the Koran.

In Christian art, the graphic, easily understood theme came to be significant. An example among thousands is a woodcut taken from Luther's German translation of the Old Testament in 1526. It illustrates Jacob's dream. But it was also interpreted as a prefiguration of, a pointer to, the ascension of Jesus. From there, in turn, it could mean the Christian's admission to heaven. The subject was sometimes simplified into a ladder and a star. The star was bliss, and the ladder was the way to it; it was an image of the soul's ascent to, or progress toward, heaven, paradise, God. The Virgin Mary was called the "ladder of heaven," because it was through her the Jesus had descended to earth and men and women could ascend to heaven.

The ladder became the attribute of a number of saints, such as Perpetua, for whom martyrdom was the way, "the ladder," to heaven. Or St. John Climacus, who formulated a whole theology of the ladder. The Christian way of life, he said, is a ladder; each rung is a good deed, a virtue, or a pious development leading us a further step upward, nearer to perfection, the climax of goodness, God. The actual Greek word for "ladder" is *klimax*, which gave him his appellation. In Latin "ladder" is *scala*, and several monasteries were called *Scala Dei*, "Ladder of God." The ladder had become a "ladder of virtue." Oddly

The angels of God ascending and descending on Jacob's ladder. But why do angels need a ladder? They have wings and can fly! They have not always had them. In the early days of Christianity angels did not have wings. They inherited them later from winged pagan gods.

enough, it could stand especially for the cardinal Christian virtue of humility. He that shall humble himself shall be exalted. "Lowliness is young ambition's ladder."

Outside the religious sphere, the ladder was taken as a symbol of upward striving, of spirit, intellect, or character and of any gradual progress in a study or a training. To scholars the ladder was an image of the whole of human knowledge, of Philosophia, with seven steps corresponding to the seven liberal arts, or of the very technique of thought, in which, as in logical reasoning, one advances step by step. To writers and poets the ladder was the way to Parnassus. To alchemists it symbolized their quest for the philosopher's stone. To all it was the way to self-improvement, the means to mental and perhaps even material advancement; it was the *Scala perfectionis*, the "ladder of perfection and perfectability."

The Candle and the Candlestick

The first thing that God did after creating the heaven and the earth was to provide light. "And God saw the light, that it was good." In this respect man agrees with God. Light means joy, security, salvation, exaltation, and deliverance. Light dispels melancholy and "darkness"; light averts evil. Fire, lamps, and torches are associated in every religion with sanctity, worship, and reverence, and this also applies to the small light that we call a candle. "Light in darkness" signifies hope. Amnesty International has for its badge a candle raising its flame above the surrounding barbed wire.

This postage stamp commemorates an event—the radio news of Denmark's liberation on May 4, 1945—whose joy could not be expressed in words. Thousands of people spontaneously lit candles and put them in their windows.

Many nations burn candles in sacred ceremonies. The ancient Romans did so at weddings. For Jews, as for Christians, candles are an almost indispensable part of divine service. In church the lighted altar candles signify the presence of God. We commemorate our dead with candles. Candles express grief, penitence, devotion.

They also express joy and festivity. At meetings of the Swedish Academy a lighted candle stands in front of each of the members. In Denmark a festive dinner is almost unthinkable without this "living light." And when the Danish radio announced on the evening of May 4, 1945 that the German occupying forces had capitulated and Denmark was free again, candles were lit spontaneously in every window, hundreds of thousands of them in minutes.

In the church year candles play a particularly important part at Easter and Candlemas, the "mass of candles." This is celebrated 40 days after the birth of Jesus, that is, on February 2, to commemorate his presentation in the temple, where the aged Simeon called him "a light that shall be revealed unto the gentiles." Whether the "light" Simeon had in mind was a candle may be doubtful, but that was the interpretation put upon it by a literal-minded posterity. The wax that melts they saw as Christ's humanity, and the flame consuming the wax as his divinity.

There was also quite another symbolism associated with the candle. It was an image of human life, and one spoke of "the light" of a person's life. In this sense candles occur, for example, in Shakespeare—"Out, out, brief candle!" (*Macbeth*)—and in Grimms' fairy tales. In the 16th century an extinguished candle became a motif on gravestones, and in 17th-century allegorical art the candle had become a symbol of the brevity of life, the corruption of the body, and Death.

The candle is also the attribute of many saints, such as St. Genevieve, whose candle the Devil blew out but which an angel lit again. She is the patron saint of Paris and of candle-makers. Fides (Truth) and Grammatica (Linguistics) are also known by their lighted candles. The latter perhaps because of the late-night studies presupposed by the study of grammar!

A candle is generally placed in a candlestick, and this, too, has a place in symbolism. To the Romans a candlestick could represent Vesta, the goddess of the hearth, the home, and chastity and at the same time Venus, in this connection doubt-less as the goddess of marriage and married love. In Christian symbolism a candlestick can stand for Mary, who bore "the light of the world." Easily the most famous of all candlesticks, however, is the seven-branched candelabrum, the Hebrew menorah. It was originally confined to the Jewish tabernacle as ordained by Moses and is fully described in chapter 25 of Exodus (where it is said to bear seven *lamps*).

Of all Jewish symbols, the seven-branched candlestick is the most characteristic and best known. Despite the Talmudic injunction against depicting it, there were representations of it in synagogues and on Jewish tombstones, it would seem, before the birth of Christ, and later it became general in Jewish ornamentation. When the Romans destroyed the temple of Herod in the year 70, they carried off the seven-branched can-delabrum to Rome. What it looked like we know exactly from the Arch of Titus in Rome, where it is shown being borne in triumph with other booty. To Jews the Menorah signifies Jahveh's protection and presence and indeed symbolizes Jehovah himself. To non-Jews it signifies Jewry, the Jews, Jewish religion, the Old Testament. In 1949 Israel placed the Menorah in its national arms. But the seven-branched candle-stick is also a Christian symbol. It appeared in ancient times in Christian churches, especially in connection with Candle-mas. In the course of the 16th century it became almost a regu-lar church fitting, in Protestant countries at any rate. It was regarded as a symbol of "the word" and "the light of the world," that is, of Christ.

To the Jews the seven branches symbolized the seven

The Menorah, the Israeli seven-branched candlestick, copied exactly from the most authentic known representation of the original on the Arch of Titus in Rome. The candlestick is flanked by two olive branches, and below them is the word "Israel" in Hebrew. All the devices are in white on a blue ground.

"lamps of heaven," meaning perhaps the seven planets. To the Christians the branches represented the seven archangels, the seven sacraments, the seven Christian virtues (stemming from a common root), and, later, especially, the seven gifts of the Holy Ghost. The seven-branched form, however, undoubtedly goes back to the Babylonian preoccupation with the number seven, starting with the seven days of the week, arrived at by quartering a lunar month from new moon to new moon (see the chapter on the holy seven). It is probable, indeed, that the whole candelabrum is of Babylonian origin and that it in fact represents or symbolizes a tree with lights, a candlelit tree. If this is correct, there is a relationship, distant but unmistakable, between the seven-branched candelabrum and another tree of light, our Christmas tree.

Amnesty International

	DANISH SECTION
A MOVEMENT TO FIGHT PERSECUTION AND PROTECT HUMAN RIGHTS	Frederiksborggade 1 1360 Copenhagen K Denmark Tlf. (01) 11 75 41

The Gridiron

In the year 258 the Roman emperor Licinius Valerianus decided to confiscate the property of the Christian communities. The clergy, including a deacon named Laurentius, were arrested, but, when told to deliver up his church's treasures, he summoned the parish poor and, pointing to them, said, "These are the Church's treasures!" Of course, this did not do him any good. Laurentius, or Lawrence, as he is called in English, was condemned to death by roasting on a red-hot gridiron. But he was still capable of another memorable rejoinder. After lying for a while on the grill he said to his executioners: "*Assatus sum* . . . I am done on this side. You can turn me."

It is no wonder that this imperturbable deacon became one of the Church's most popular saints. Stories about him, of his generosity to the poor, and not least of his courage on the red-hot grill, were told all over Europe. In Spain he was believed to be a Spaniard, and with St. James he became the national saint. His death on the grid had taken place on August 10, and, when Philip II of Spain won a victory over the French in the Battle of St. Quentin on that date in 1557, he decided to build a palace in honor of St. Lawrence. This was the Escorial, northwest of Madrid, built between 1563 and 1584, the largest Renaissance palace in the world and regarded by Spaniards as the eighth wonder of the world. The palace has 16 courtyards, and its ground plan has the form of a gridiron, the one St. Lawrence died on.

Another place where Lawrence was particularly popular was Scandinavia. He was the patron saint of the first Scandinavian archbishopric, that of Lund; numerous Danish and Swedish churches are dedicated to him; and his grid can still be seen in the arms of a number of towns and cities. The Scandinavian form of Laurentius is Lars, and the surname Larsen, or Larsson, is one of the commonest in Scandinavia: "Hr. Larsen" is the Danish equivalent of "John Doe." In primitive medieval calendars the picture for August 10 is the gridiron of St. Lawrence. At this time of year there are exceptionally many shooting stars in the night sky in Denmark, and they are called "the tears of St. Lawrence."

Clearly, a man who had been grilled to death was an expert in such things. St. Lawrence therefore gave protection against fires, burns, and scalding while also being the patron saint of firemen, charcoal burners, and—with a robust jollity corresponding to his own stoicism on the gridiron—eating-house keepers, restaurateurs, chefs, and bakers. He figures, gridiron in hand, in guild signs and on trade-union banners. Whether this is really a symbol is debatable, but I think the story is worth telling.

A 16th-century seal with gridiron for a Swedish church, one of many churches in Sweden and Denmark dedicated to St. Lawrence.

Receptacles

Bowls and Jugs

Domestic vessels—bowls, jugs, and other pots—are significant symbols, sometimes in themselves but even more by what they are imagined to contain. In the latter case it is usually immaterial whether the vessel is a bowl or jug or any other pot. The point is what is in it. It can be water, oil, milk, and much else, but it can also be something even harder to represent, such as the grace of God. It is the purpose of symbols to express something impalpable by means of something concrete, and in a way this is doubly so in the case of receptacle symbols.

Doubtless it all began with offerings to the gods. They might be animals or fruit, but the costliest gifts were often liquid—oil, wine, milk, honey—and they could best be presented in a bowl or jug. Such offerings were a daily feature in both Greek and Roman religious practice, and a bowl became in time the visual manifestation of sacrifice, worship, devotion, and piety. Altars were decorated with reliefs of bowls; gods were pictured with a bowl. The bowl from which her sacred temple serpents were fed their milk became the fixed attribute of Hygeia, the Greek goddess of health and hygiene. She appears occasionally today on pharmacy signs, identifiable by the serpent and bowl. Sometimes there will have been soup or other cooked foods in the sacrificial vessel, perhaps with a view to a ritual meal, a meal of atonement between men and gods. Possibly the jugs and bowls of beer, soup, and gruel found in prehistoric graves in Scandinavia and elsewhere had a similar purpose.

Thus the bowl stood for human donations to the gods. But it also symbolized God's gifts to man. This was especially so of God's grace, which "rains" and "flows" and "floweth over." A bowl or jug is often seen on Jewish gravestones, and the same subject is common in the wall paintings of Roman catacombs from the first centuries of Christianity. There the *Vas Christi*, or "vessel of Christ," symbolized his inexhaustible grace. Of all God's gifts in fluid form, water is the commonest and cheapest but at the same time the most precious. No water, no life. With water come life, fertility, crops, abundance, benediction, refreshment, cleansing, cleanness. That is what, for instance, christening water and holy water is (or was) meant to say.

Aquarius, the water carrier, the eleventh sign of the zodiac, is usually shown with one or two pitchers. In Babylon it was he who opened the sluices of the rainy season. Medieval woodcut.

A German church fresco, c. 1250, depicting the formation of the river Euphrates, according to Genesis.

All this and much more came to be symbolized in the water jug. The jug stood for the source of life, for fertilization, fertility, rebirth, renewal, resurrection, salvation, eternal life. It could also quite simply stand for *aqua*, water in the scientific sense as one of the four elements. And a jug was usually an attribute of Aquarius, the water carrier, the eleventh sign of the zodiac. He reigns from January 20 to February 19, the period that in his Babylonian homeland is the rainy season. It is Aquarius with the jug who opens the sluices of heaven and waters the tree of life.

But it was not only water in general that the jug contained. It symbolized specific great waters: the four rivers of paradise (including the Euphrates and Tigris), the Nile, the Tiber. A reclining old man holding a jug symbolized a river. The jug could stand or lie, with the water pouring from it, or the old man might be pouring it. River gods, water gods, sea gods—Oceanus, the ocean, had his jug, and in the Renaissance and baroque periods the image spread to the whole of Europe. A jug could in time stand for any waterway at all.

Water gushes forth. It flows over. Or you pour it out. You do not do that with olive oil. Every drop is valuable, and usually the jug is closed with a lid. Oil was used for cooking but also as a medicine, not least for external application, for cleansing and "anointing." As a symbol the jug of oil stands for consecration, ritual cleansing, remission of sins. As an attribute it identifies Samuel, who anointed Saul, and the two saints of medicine, Cosmas and Damianus. A woman with an anointing vessel

Father Sound, with his pitcher and a harpoon, watching as the coast is surveyed near Elsinore. Danish engraving, 1775.

will nearly always represent Mary Magdalene, "a woman in the city," "a sinner," who anointed the feet of Jesus. She is the patron saint of "fallen women."

There are other vessels. One containing soup is the attribute of the prophet Habakkuk. If the contents are an infusion of herbs, the jug symbolizes the archangel Raphael, the patron saint of pharmacists. A jug of colors can indicate St. Luke, who

A jar with a lid must be for oil or ointment, and a woman with an anointing jug must be Mary Magdalene. Here, elegantly dressed and with her hair nicely plaited, is the beautiful sinner who visited Jesus in the house of Pharisees and anointed his feet. Fresco from c. 1500 in the church at Kirke Stillinge in Denmark.

is supposed to have been a painter. Unless he is holding the vessel up in front of him, as if to see through it, in which case the "jug" is more likely a urine flask, which is also an attribute of Luke, since he is thought also to have been a physician. Other jugs hold vinegar, myrrh, manna, potpourri.

What of the wine jug? Wine must also have had significance. It did. Immense significance. But with one exception symbolic wine vessels seem to be confined to cups, drinking bowls, or chalices. It is a vast subject but very different from the jug. The single exception of a symbolical wine jug is, ironically enough, associated with Temperantia, the goddess of temperance and moderation. She is identifiable by her two vessels, whose contents she is mixing. One holds wine, the other water, with which she is diluting the wine in order to avoid being intoxicated.

The Horn of Plenty

"It will all be the same a hundred years hence." That is one way of saying that time is mightier than all else. Even the greatest works of man and of nature are outmatched by time; sooner or later they come to nothing, and only time endures. "Time devours his own children."

In Greek mythology the idea was personified in the god of time, Kronos, or Cronus (from whose name we get "chronometer" and "chronology"), who literally devoured his children when they were born. On one occasion, however, he was worsted. When his wife (and sister) Rhea, or Earth, was about to give birth yet again, she made up her mind this time to save the infant. She wrapped up a rock to resemble a baby and gave it to Cronus, who swallowed it. Then she fled to Crete and there gave birth to the infant god Zeus. In Crete Zeus was suckled by a goat, Amalthea, and later, after he had overcome his father and become master of the world, Zeus showed his gratitude to his foster mother by admitting her to the firmament as a constellation and turning one of her horns into a wonderful "cornucopia," or horn of plenty. It had the quality of being inexhaustible in all the good and beautiful things that man could imagine: fruits and cereals and flowers, food and drink, and all that was delectable on earth.

In the mythological account this horn finished up with the river god Akeloos. But in art it soon became an attribute also of other river gods, as well as a symbol of what the great rivers brought: fertility, crops, prosperity, commerce, and riches. And not only river gods. From the horn flowed all the products of agriculture, commerce, and industry, all the blessings of peace, all the rewards of diligence, hope, charity, and goodness. The corresponding gods and goddesses were invariably shown with the bounteous horn, and so it is no wonder that the cornucopia, or horn of plenty, became one of the most universal themes of Greek and Roman art. It was usually represented as a large, twisted cornet.

With the Renaissance the horn of plenty was taken up in European art, and it soon became as universal as it had been in classical times. No picture of the wealth of nations, no glorification of royal achievements was without it. It was plainly a

Cash is raining from the cornucopia, so the woman surely personifies commerce and its blessings. Her shawl is borne aloft by the wind, she is pointing to the seas, and one can easily imagine a similar image used as the figurehead of a ship in the mercantile period.

device that had popular appeal. It also appealed to the New World. The hope of colonists and pioneers of the riches the new country and their own efforts would bring them was often illustrated with a cornucopia filled with fruits, flowers, minerals, or gold coins. There are horns of plenty in the state seals of Idaho and Wisconsin and in the national arms of Honduras, Panama, Colombia, Venezuela, and Peru.

Alongside the traditional allegory common to the West Danes have given to the wondrous horn a role and an elaboration that may be unique. In Danish a "horn of plenty" usually means the large, cornet-shaped almond confection that concludes a banquet and allows a pile of chocolates and marzipan, toys and knickknacks to flow out on to the table. No christening, wedding party, or, especially, confirmation-day dinner is complete without a cornucopia, the gift of Zeus to man. A similar custom is practiced in Latin America. A *piñata*, a paper horn filled with goodies, is broken open by children on their saint's days.

Commerce

Scales

Really to understand how something works—how, say, a machine or a piece of equipment functions—is one of the deep satisfactions of life. Such a profound satisfaction occurs in watching a pair of scales balance exactly. The experience appeals not only to the intellect but also to the emotions. We feel that weighing is not just something physical but that it can be moral and ethical as well.

In every civilization that has known scales the clear, beautiful device has indeed been used as an image both of something tangible and of something intangible. Scales, of course, symbolize the people and the occupations that weigh: grocers, pharmacists, and, by extension, trade and commerce in general. In this sense scales occur in thousands of allegorical settings. They can also symbolize honesty and have been used in the trademarks of auditing firms. It is not only people who weigh. God weighs people; God weighs our deeds. "For the Lord is a God of knowledge, and by him actions are weighed," we are told in the Book of Samuel. "Let me be weighed in an

Let righteousness be our guide, because God weighs our actions! The scales of God against a ruined landscape, a 17th-century woodcut illustrating Proverbs 10:2-3.

even balance, that God may know mine integrity," Job says. The most famous symbol of weighing, however, must be that of Daniel interpreting the writing on the wall for Belshazzar, the king of Babylon: "Thou art weighed in the balances, and art found wanting."

This Old Testament symbol of weighing had its precursors in Egypt, where "weighing of souls," the final assessment of a man's good and bad deeds, was a permanent part of the testing to which everyone was subjected after death. The weighing of souls is described exactly in the Egyptian *Book of the Dead* and represented countless times in the murals of tombs. On a huge pair of scales, set between Osiris seated on his throne on one side and on the other the monsters of the Underworld, Anubis weighs the dead person's soul. And does so exactly! Sometimes he uses a feather as a counterweight.

Christianity also refers to the weighing of souls. God on the Day of Judgment, holding his scales, is depicted in several places in the catacombs. Later the weighing of souls devolved on the archangel Michael, often shown standing between God and the open jaws of Hell, between reward and punishment, salvation or damnation. The result depended on the weighing. The construction parallels the Egyptian pictures exactly, but there is apparently no direct connection. The theme became extremely popular during the Middle Ages and can be seen in hundreds of churches and chapels. St. Michael became the patron saint of all weighers—grocers, pharmacists, bakers, and the like.

Scales also occurred in Greek mythology. They belonged to Zeus, who usually delegated the weighing of souls to a minor god, such as Hermes. Hermes, who corresponds to the Roman Mercury, is chiefly known as the god of commerce, and it may be possible that the scales were the origin of his function. The scales of Zeus, however, also represent something else. All over the world where scales have been used—China, India, Tibet, Persia, the Near East—the beam with two pans has primarily symbolized equilibrium, equity, equipoise, equality (notably before the law), equal rights, justice. The symbol is almost universal: it is used in the Koran, and it was used in the French Revolution.

To the Greeks scales were a symbol of the balance of nature and of social balance. They symbolized "fair dealing," weighing of arguments, administration of justice, fair judgment. Generally it was the goddess Themis, identifiable by her scales, who represented Zeus as the defender of justice. She was not nearly as well known, however, as the Roman Justitia, who became one of the most familiar symbols of white civilization. She is often shown holding a pair of scales in one hand and a sword in the other. Together they mean equality before the law, weighing of the evidence, and thereafter just punishment. From the Renaissance she was usually blindfolded, symbolizing the impartiality of the court and the guarantee of fair treatment, because she could not look to either side. On the other hand, if it is God's justice that is illustrated, the figure is not blindfolded, because God's justice is not blind.

Scales and sword or scales by themselves became a symbol

The archangel Michael as a weigher of souls and killer of dragons. Man's soul is seen in the pan on the right, while in the pan on the left are his sins in the shape of a millstone, heavy and massive but not heavy enough to outweigh the soul. German printer's mark, 1519.

of judicial practice, legal knowledge, jurisprudence, the study of law, the judicial system, and law enforcement. Interpol has a pair of scales in its emblem. It is not only lawyers, however, who have to "weigh up" a matter and "weigh" their words. Scales became a general symbol of assessment for and against, of discernment, sound judgment, prudence, temperance, equanimity, "poise," "everything in moderation." And in addition, from the same point of departure but with a quite different result, of doubt and of the art of disputation, dialectics, and logical argument.

Scales were seen everywhere, even in the sky. The name for the constellation of the Scales (Libra) can be traced back to the Babylonians, who divided the sun's yearly course across the firmament into twelve phases, naming them after constellations (see the chapter on the Zodiac). It is a measure of the symbolic power of scales that they were the only nonliving member of the zodiac. The phase was from September 23 to October 23, and the placing can scarcely have been accidental. September 23 is the autumnal equinox when day and night are of equal length all over the world.

Merchandising, honesty, weighing of souls, the Day of Judgment, justice, equality before the law, the balance of day and night—scales can mean all these things, sometimes several of them at the same time, and it can be hard to tell which came first. In medieval calendars a pair of scales was the picture for September 29. Was this because it was the date fixed by the Church for celebrating St. Michael, the weigher of souls? Or was it because it was in the phase of Libra, the Scales? Is there a link between the weighing of souls by the archangel and the constellation of the Babylonians?

Farmer's calendar from Austria for September 1398. The last picture above, corresponding to September 29, represents the scales of Michael.

The Postal Horn

To most people on the continent of Europe the picture of a certain wind instrument—an almost circular tube with a large, open bell—indicates something to do with postal services, for example, a post office. It says, "Here you can buy stamps, remit a money order, or dispatch a parcel." It is an ordinary, everyday sign and yet is far from self-evident. It means nothing to people from the other side of the world or even from Britain, where it is not used as a post-office sign. There is no apparent connection—in logic or association—between the functions of the postal services and a musical instrument. Of course, there is an explanation, but it is historical: that of the coachman who, by blowing his horn, announced that letters could be collected and dispatched. Without this historical knowledge the post-office horn is inexplicable.

But not meaningless. A symbol is not there to be "read." A symbol is a device showing one thing but meaning another. And one does not have to be able to deduce this other thing. A cap symbolizes liberty, an anchor hope, a dove peace or sanctity, a serpent medicine, and a horseshoe good luck. They are all familiar symbols, and we all know what they mean. But in no case can we infer their meaning.

When the post offices in time encompassed other jobs in addition to carrying letters, officials wanted to give these new aspects of the service pictorial expression in its emblem. The telegraph service was given two flashes of lightning, later replaced by two arrows—Telegraph messengers sped like an arrow! But technology changes even faster, and in the winter of 1973–74 the Danish Postal and Telegraph Service announced a competition for a new emblem intended also to illustrate newer "forms of telecommunication."

Anyone who is up to date, however, soon becomes out of date. Today telecommunications, tomorrow satellites. And the day after tomorrow perhaps beams, particles, telepathic post. If an emblem is to keep in step, it has to be changed continually. But it should not be. Quite functionally, there is no reason why it should. A horn has stood hitherto for the post office, unintelligible (without historical studies) and yet altogether effective. A horn can stand just as effectively for the telegraph service or telecommunications or whatever else the future may bring. A symbol is not intended for reason: it is meant for the eye.

The Wheel

The first wheels created by man, 5,000 to 6,000 years ago, must have made an overwhelming impression. First because of the way they advanced: by rotating around themselves, quite unlike any other movement in nature. Secondly—as the construction became lighter, with spokes and rims—by the marvelous speed they made. The vehicle was winged! The wheel became a symbol of speed, haste, "flight." In modern times, when wheels had become an everyday sight and no longer made such a deep impression, wings would sometimes be added to emphasize the "flying speed."

More important, however, than the speed of the wheel was its manner of moving. The wheel came to symbolize "perpetual" motion, ending and recommencing, nothing being permanent but everything returning. The wheel illustrated "rotation," the cycle of cosmic mechanics, the regular changes and "course" of life and nature. To be "bound to the wheel" meant to be dependent on the laws of the universe. Indian philosophy speaks of the "doctrine of the wheel": that is, of the regular law of everything that no one can escape. The wheel plays a significant part among both Hindus and Buddhists, and Dharma Tshakra, the "Wheel of Life," is in the Indian national flag and coat of arms.

The wheel symbolizes the year's course, the course of life, and the course of the world. The Epistle of James in the New

A Danish version of the wheel of fortune. On one side of the great revolving wheel a man is ascending toward splendor, glory, and power. At the top of the wheel he sits enthroned holding a glass of wine, smiled on by fortune, but for how long? On the other side of the wheel he has been toppled from the peak of success. And below the wheel he is a beggar. Fresco painting, c. 1480, in Tingsted Church in Denmark.

Testament, in some translations, speaks of "the wheel of life," and the Rosicrucians, 1,500 years later, of "the world's wheel." The fact that the sun is shaped like a wheel and seems to move in the same way undoubtedly contributed to this extensive complex of symbolism.

The irregular changes of nature and human life can also be symbolized by the wheel. Where a rolling wheel will end cannot be easily predicted. So the wheel became a symbol both of a person's inconstancy, instability, fickleness, restlessness, and unrest and of the changing fortunes of all human life, of upheavals and vicissitudes; of the freaks of fortune and the surprises of fate.

This latter idea was expressed in particular by the symbol of the "wheel of fortune" or the "wheel of life." The concept derives from antiquity, but as a concrete, visual picture it seems to have first taken shape in the Middle Ages. On one side of the great, rotating wheel man is on the way up, toward luxury, glory, and power. At the top of the wheel sits a king, smiled on by fortune, but for how long? On the other side of the wheel men are going down and in the end are unable to hold on and fall off and are crushed. The graphic allegory was very popular and is found all over Europe. That there is still a link between "wheel" and "fortune" is shown by the "wheel of fortune" of the fairground and the roulette wheel of the casino.

Sometimes the wheel did not turn by itself but was kept revolving by Fortuna, the goddess of good fortune or destiny. A wheel became one of her attributes from the Renaissance, usually in such a way that she would be shown balancing on a wheel (or a ball, which eventually became the most common).

Destiny can mean two things: the inevitable ("no one can escape his fate") and the unforeseeable ("the whims of fate"). Fortuna balancing on the revolving wheel, of course, meant its whims but was also mistakenly regarded as "the inevitable." This led to the interpretation of the wheel as Nemesis,

Ezekiel's wheel, woodcut in a Danish bible, 1589. The four creatures on the left with eagle, human, ox, and lion heads have also played a big role in symbolism.

punitive justice, deserved retribution that sooner or later overtakes the guilty. Interestingly enough, the Indian wheel of Karma, "the wheel that crushes," can mean something similar: the destructive forces of life, the relentlessness of existence. Occasio, "the favorable moment" that had to be seized as one stops a revolving wheel, could be identified by the wheel. Oddly enough, it is often shown lying flat, with Occasio standing on it, whereby the picture becomes meaningless.

A quite different wheel is spoken of by the prophet Ezekiel: "Behold one wheel upon the earth . . . and . . . as it were a wheel in the middle of a wheel." These wheels, sometimes with wings or eyes, are a significant feature of his visions, but what they mean is not clear. To the archbishop of Mainz in Germany, however, Ezekiel's wheel was the "wheel (or carriage) of God," *Currus Dei*. He took this designation as one of the titles of his office, placing the "wheel of God" in the arms of the archdiocese.

From there it rolled on. The archbishop was a mighty man, one of the seven electoral princes of the German Empire, with widespread possessions and thousands of people in his service. Many of the towns that the archdiocese embraced and many of the families that earned their livelihood there took a variation of the archepiscopal wheel as their coat of arms. And that is, if not the only reason, one of the most important reasons why the wheel appears today in the arms of hundreds of German municipalities and families and is one of the commonest devices in the whole of German heraldry.

Another heraldic wheel is that of St. Catherine, who was put to death by means of a wheel. Her popularity was immense, and she is the patron saint of all who have to do with wheels: carters, wheelwrights, spinners, millers, and cyclists.

Figures

If two equilateral triangles are laid one over the other, one with its apex pointing upward and the other with it pointing down, the result is a beautiful and fascinating device, especially when the two triangles are interlaced. The device has many names, including "hexagram."

The hexagram is very ancient as an ornamentation and a magic sign over large parts of the earth: in the Orient, in Africa, and in Europe. Muslims call it "Solomon's seal," and until 1960 it formed a part of the national arms of Nigeria. It also figures in the national symbolism of Ethiopia. In Europe the device was employed by goldsmiths and alchemists with various mean-

The hexagram, or star of David, is one of the most aesthetically and psychologically satisfying devices in existence. It has been popular in many nations over much of the world but has chiefly been known as a Jewish symbol.

ings, such as "prime matter" (*prima materia*), the soul, God.

In Hebrew the device is called the "shield of David" or the "star of David." It appears on Jewish tombstones and other archaeological finds dating back to the 7th century B.C. When the Jews were driven out of Palestine by the Romans, they took the star of David with them, perhaps as a reminder of the Jewish kingdom and a sign of the guardianship of God. When Zionism was organized in the 1890s, it took the star of David as its official emblem; and, when the state of Israel was proclaimed in 1947, it included it in the national flag. (The national arms display the seven-branched candelabrum).

Long before then the device had been accepted by non-Jews as a symbol of Jews and Jewry. In the Middle Ages a yellow star of David was one of the signs of identity that the Church ordered Jews to wear so that their Christian fellow citizens might avoid them. The command went out of use or was revoked in the course of the 17th and 18th centuries. Later the star of David formed part of the hateful propaganda of antisemitism; and, when the Nazis came to power in Germany, it was universally reintroduced as a "badge of shame" for Jews in 1941. The measure was also applied in the countries Germany occupied, but some, like Denmark, succeeded in avoiding its implementation, and this is one of the few things dating from the occupation that the Danes can look back on with joy.

The Cross

The cross symbolizes Christianity. If one knows nothing else about symbols, at least one knows that. And so it does. But it does more than that. The cross had a long and independent life before Christianity came into existence and has also had a non-Christian life since, although there is no denying that Christianity took over the cross—like so much else from other religions.

The cross with four arms of equal length is undoubtedly one of the oldest symbols in the world. It has survived on ancient works of man practically everywhere—in China, in Africa, in America. In Mesopotamia the cross was a common device 2,000 years or more before the birth of Christ. It appears on

Scandinavian rock engravings dating from the Bronze Age, that is, from about 1500 B.C. The Celts on certain occasions painted crosses on their foreheads and hands.

The two short lines intersecting at right angles, "straight" or oblique, may often have been no more than an ornament. It was a fine figure, and it was easy to draw. But just as often it was doubtless regarded as a magic sign. The device would fascinate: the two crossed strokes would be more than strokes and would "mean" something, giving protection, bringing good luck, averting evil. They still do. A charm shaped like a cross will put the Devil and witches to flight, as everyone knows. The priest or clergyman makes the sign of the cross over the newly baptized infant (the two motions of the hand, together forming a cross, would seem to be older than Christianity). Belligerents do not fire on persons, vehicles, or buildings marked with the Red Cross.

A quite different survival, almost to the present day, of the cross as a magic sign is its use as a signature by persons who cannot write. They marked a cross, and this was their bond. The cross embodied their identity and their obligation. The cross on a ballot sheet to this day has a similar connotation.

So much for the decorative and the magical. What of the "meaning" in a further sense? Did the earliest crosses also represent or symbolize something? Some people have thought that the crosses in rock engravings were solar symbols. If such crosses were enclosed in a circle, the whole device resembling a wheel with four spokes, they may well be regarded as a picture, or symbol, of the sun. On the other hand, I do not think that crosses alone, without circles, are solar symbols. There are no "spokes" in the sun, and to represent the "sun's wheel" while omitting the most important feature,

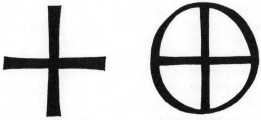

Two of the oldest symbols in the world, the Greek cross and the wheel cross.

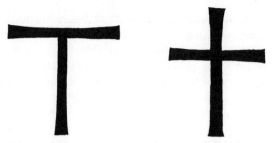

The T cross, also known as the tau or St. Anthony cross, and the Latin cross.

the disk, seems altogether meaningless, rather like trying to convey an idea of an apple by drawing the core.

But if the cross is not a solar symbol, it is probably a symbol of the world. There can scarcely be any doubt that the pre-Christian or non-Christian cross often illustrates the four corners of the world, the four quarters of the globe, and thereby becomes a picture of the "whole world." In this sense the cross was used, among others, in Amerindian civilizations before the arrival of the white man. On Assyrian reliefs dating from 1000 B.C. or earlier the cross is the attribute of celestial or universal gods. In the centuries prior to and just after the birth of Christ crosses and cross charms were common in the Near East and the classical world. They stood for the cosmos, the world, universal rule, and the protection of the cosmic powers. Their extent and importance doubtless contributed to the triumph of the Christian cross. But only after an interval.

The instrument of torture and execution on which Jesus died was called in Latin a *crux*. The word itself illustrates its cruel function: it is like a sound picture of breaking bones. In modern European languages the word developed into *cruz, croix, Kreuz,* and *cross*. But it is far from certain that the Roman instrument was shaped like what we normally think of as a cross. It may simply have been a stake. Perhaps it had a crosspiece so that the whole object looked like a T. Such "T crosses" appear in some crucifixion scenes (though, like every other picture of Christ's crucifixion, they were all done many hundreds of years after the event). Perhaps it was a cross with a crosspiece, what we understand by a cross today. The Bible gives no help. The words used in the original texts mean no more than "tree" or "stake."

In the two centuries after the death of Jesus it is doubtful that the Christians ever used the device of the cross. If they did, it was very rarely. And it is understandable. The cross of Jesus, to them, must have chiefly denoted death and evil, like the guillotine or the electric chair to later generations. Or the sign of the cross may have been regarded as pagan. About 200 A.D., there is a statement by a Christian author, Minucius Felix, who says: "We Christians neither want nor worship crosses as the pagans do." In the course of the 3rd century the pattern changed. Increasingly the Christian communities used "covert" crosses, which have survived in the murals of the catacombs and on tombstones. They might be an anchor with a crosspiece, a ship with a mast and yard, a human figure with outstretched arms, or a juxtaposition of the initials of the name Jesus or Christ (in Greek or Latin) to give a crosslike device.

The decisive change came, however, after the accession to the throne of the Emperor Constantine in the year 306. In 312 he advanced with his army against another contender, and in a vision or dream before the battle he saw a Christian symbol, and it was revealed to him that "in this sign shalt thou conquer." Constantine conquered, and the emblem concerned was introduced on the standards of the Roman army. Whether it was a cross is open to doubt. It was more likely a form of Christ's monogram, a combination of the Greek letters X and P corresponding to the Latin Ch and R. But in the following year Constantine introduced freedom of religion in the Roman Empire. The Christians no longer needed to live in concealment and disguise their cross symbols. During the 4th century the cross became an openly Christian symbol, and

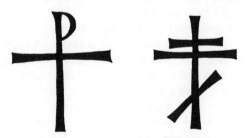

Cross-shaped monogram of Christ and Russian cross used by the Orthodox Church.

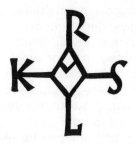

The signature of Charlemagne, Carolus, arranged as a cross. He is believed to have personally "written" only the central rectangle, with the rest added by a more literate chancellor.

in the following centuries it came to predominate. It must have been an important contributing factor that crucifixion as a method of state execution had been abolished by the Emperor Theodosius (379-95) so that the cross ceased to have the former cruel and negative associations.

The cross stood for Christ's suffering and death, but more particularly it symbolized his resurrection, triumph, power, and man's salvation. To the individual Christian the cross was a sign of faith, proclaiming "I am a Christian," but also often a protection to ward off demons. The dividing line between the contemporary Christian and non-Christian charms shaped like crosses is hard to define. To the Church the cross was a sign of benediction, consecration, "depaganizing," and property, while also representing the Christian faith and every aspect of the Christian message. It came to stand for divine service, church attendance, and, in more recent times, "Sunday" in timetables and "church" on maps. To the emperors the cross was a sign of victory and good fortune. In the 5th century they placed a cross at the top of their crowns, and later a cross replaced the figure of the goddess of victory on the royal orb. In art the cross became an attribute, by the 4th century, of the apostle Peter and later of a countless number of other saints. Christian people had a cross placed on their tombstones, and thus in time the cross came to stand for Death: today, for example, in announcements of deaths and as an entirely neutral indication, irrespective of the deceased person's religion, in genealogical and other literature.

Throughout the Middle Ages and later the shape of the cross was copied in innumerable contexts: from monograms, badges, ornaments, patterns, and trinkets to the ground plans of cathedrals. And through church art and ecclesiastical insignia, processional crosses, and the like a long succession of variants of the cross developed. The original cross, with four arms of equal length, was chiefly used, for example, in the eastern half of the Roman Empire and so was called the "Greek" cross. It is included today in the national flag and arms of Greece. The cross in the Swiss flag and arms is also a Greek cross. It was transmitted (in reversed colors) to the Red Cross flag and from it in turn (again with other colors) was taken up by first-aid groups, pharmaceutical firms, and dealers in nursing appliances. The oblique cross of St. Andrew appears in the flag of Scotland and in the Union flag of Britain and before 1917 was included in the Russian flag. There are some 300 or more "recognized" and named types of cross. Some— St. Anthony's cross, the Maltese cross, the Celtic cross, the cross of Lorraine, and the ankh—are widely known. But the possible variants are endless. Incidentally, the pre-Christian symbolism of the cross lived on. The poet Dante refers to the cross, for example, as a picture of the universe. But this concept can hardly have been widely diffused.

A special role in the symbolism and evolution of the cross was played by the crusades from 1095 A.D. to the end of the 13th century. They stimulated the institution of military fraternities such as the Knights Templars and the Order of St. John of Jerusalem, each of which had a cross of a special shape and color. The medieval knightly fraternities were copied in orders of chivalry, in which in time the most important feature was the device or figure of a cross that the members were permitted to wear. And the orders of chivalry developed in turn into the whole system of civil orders and war decorations: the knight's, commander's, and grand commander's cross; orders of merit; medals for long and faithful service; the Navy Cross, Victoria Cross, the Iron Cross, the Distinguished Flying Cross, and so on.

The Ankh

In church art one sometimes sees a cross of which the upper part is shaped like a ring, loop, or handle. The same device is found in Egyptian art a thousand years or more before the birth of Christ, and no tourist in the Muslim Egypt of today can help but see the "ankh" there, too, possibly used as a charm but in any case as a ubiquitous tourist souvenir.

There is no argument about what the device means or meant. In ancient Egyptian art it stood for respiration, life, resuscitation, and perhaps especially life after death, eternal life. It was an almost permanent accessory of benign gods and goddesses, those that were on the side of man and of life. As a rule they are shown holding the device by its "handle." It is present everywhere in Egyptian tomb paintings and is found in large numbers in the form of cast charms. When Christianity reached Egypt, the Coptic communities transmitted the device. It was almost identical to the Christian cross, and, in regard to the meaning, it was not a far cry to the resurrection

The loving goddess in the middle, with the ankh cross over her arm, is pleading for the dead soul in front of Osiris, while the monster of the Underworld lurks below. Egyptian tomb painting, c. 1100 B.C.

and everlasting life of Christianity. At any rate the beautiful figure lived on. The ankh is common on early Christian tombstones in the Nile valley, and from Egypt it spread to the rest of Christendom.

That is what the device meant. What it originally represented is another story, and this is debated. A sandal thong, the Egyptian-English dictionary says, but this explanation is rejected by a Danish egyptologist, who thinks that the device represents a royal or divine headdress, a frontlet with three pendent ends. The Egyptian word *ankh*, which means "life" and which gives the device its name, also means "wreath." Other people think that the device represents a magic knot or loop or a sacred belt. Still others regard it as a stylized representation of the female genitals (the womb) and point to the similarity to the "mirror of Venus." It is not far from "life" to "love," at any rate. Finally, there are those who see the device as an implement, a "Nile key": a key or a handle for opening or closing the dams in the Nile system of dikes and canals—that is, for controlling the water that was the precondition of all life in Egypt.

The Cross of Lorraine

When Jesus was crucified, Pontius Pilate caused a notice to be set up over his head with the words: "This is Jesus, the King of the Jews." Pictures of Christ's cross with this inscription developed into a cross device with an extra set of (smaller) arms above the two customary ones, and this device had a distinctive career: it came eventually to be regarded as a special symbol of the struggle against the enemies of Christendom or of man.

One of the leaders of the First Crusade was the French magnate Godfrey of Bouillon, Duke of Lorraine, who in 1099 captured Jerusalem from the Saracens. Godfrey's standard in the fighting against the infidels is thought to have displayed a double cross as just described; at any rate he and his successors as dukes of Lorraine were later credited with this emblem, and that is how the device got its name. The arms of Hungary also contained a double cross, and there, too, it came to symbolize the struggle against the hereditary enemy of the

Christians, the Turks.

When the International Union for the Campaign against Tuberculosis, in the 1920s, wanted an emblem that would characterize its work, it chose the cross of Lorraine to indicate that the campaign was a modern "crusade." In some countries tuberculosis sanatoria are supported by the revenue from Christmas seals, and that is why Godfrey of Bouillon's cross can often be seen on letters and parcels at Christmas. The United States, Sweden, Finland, and Holland are among the countries concerned.

When Charles de Gaulle laid the foundations of the Free French forces in London in 1940, he chose the cross of Lorraine as their emblem, also, it would appear, because he thought (wrongly) that Joan of Arc had the same device in her banner 500 years before when she drove the enemy (then the English) out of France. To the Free French the cross of Lorraine indicated that their struggle against the Germans was a crusade, a holy war. They used it everywhere, above all in the Tricolor itself, and soon the emblem was also employed by the Resistance Movement in France. The device was easy to draw in three strokes, and it could be painted on a German barracks or scratched on a military vehicle in seconds.

After the war the cross of Lorraine was included in war decorations and memorials, and at the same it gradually became the Gaullist party badge. When de Gaulle came to

The calligraphic lion was probably meant as a tribute to Duke Francis of Lorraine, who in 1736 married the Habsburg princess, later empress, Maria Theresa. With one paw the lion is supporting the Habsburg Austrian shield; with the other it is holding the cross of Lorraine.

power in 1959, he incorporated the cross of Lorraine in his presidential flag. It had, as it were, become his personal emblem, the symbol of his struggle and triumph. Under Pompidou it was not seen so often, and under Giscard d'Estaing it has almost disappeared. But it is hardly dead. The cross of Lorraine merely awaits its next crusade.

The Mirror of Venus

Some of the best parts of our natural-history lessons at school were spent studying the various creatures preserved in spirit in glass jars or, even better, standing stuffed on their little wooden pedestals. They would be labeled with their names, and usually there would be a small sign indicating their sex that we soon learned to decipher. A circle with a small arrow pointing obliquely upward stood for "male." And a circle with a small cross below it meant "female." The latter device is called the "mirror of Venus," we were told; a name suggesting a different application. The fact is that the two devices, besides their use in zoology (and botany) to indicate male and female, are also employed in astronomy, where they stand for the planets Mars and Venus, as well as in chemistry and metallurgy, where they mean iron and copper. How does all this connect?

The planets Mars and Venus were named after two of the most important divinities in Roman mythology, Mars, the god of war, and Venus, the goddess of love. When the astronomers or astrologers (who were often one and the same) of the Middle Ages and Renaissance had to insert the names of planets

in their observations or horoscopes, they would employ a special sign rather than spell the names out. In the cases of Mars and Venus they used the two devices already mentioned: the circle with an arrow and the circle with a cross.

The fact that the Mars device was also used to denote "iron" was probably due to the fact that Mars chiefly used iron for making his arms: sword and spear, helmet and mail coat. Without iron Mars is of little worth; iron is to a marked degree his metal. The link between the Venus device and copper has another explanation. Venus entered the world in Cyprus, and in classical times that was where copper chiefly came from. The very word "copper" and the name "Cyprus" stem from the same root. So copper was the metal of Venus. What of biology? Here the explanation must be that the two divinities, Mars and Venus, the warrior and the queen of love, were regarded as being so typical of their respective sexes that the signs that symbolized them as individual gods or planets came also to denote the sex itself and all other creatures of the same sex.

The name "mirror of Venus" points in the same direction. The device had to have an explanation, like everything else. And as the round disk with what looks like a handle under it can suggest a hand mirror and since Venus, as the embodiment of all that is feminine, may be assumed to take pleasure in looking in the glass, the device was simply called the "mirror of Venus." There is another explanation, however. At any rate, one scholar believes that the device, somehow or another, was originally a representation of the female genitals. But it is more likely that the ring-plus-cross is a botched, later stylized representation of the Greek letters for "phs," which is an abbreviation of *phosphoros,* the "luminous one," an admiring appellative for Venus both as a planet and as a goddess.

Very recently the beautiful old device that is so easy to reproduce and recognize has taken on a completely new lease of life as a symbol and campaign badge of Women's Lib. Often it is used by itself but sometimes with an addition that is intended to emphasize its meaning. It may be seen with an equals sign placed in the circle, a nice way of saying, "We women are of equal value with men, and we claim equal conditions." Usually, however, the addition is much less "nice" but on the other hand more striking. It consists of a fist placed ın the middle of the mirror of Venus. What that means nobody can doubt. One can almost hear the clink of broken glass.

The Dollar Sign

To the ancient Greeks the straits of Gibraltar were the end of the world. Beyond them there was only the trackless ocean and then nothing. The two headlands flanking the straits, the rock of Gibraltar to the north and the Jebel Muza to the south, had, according to Greek mythology, been put there by Hercules when he was performing his famous twelve labors in those parts, and the Pillars of Hercules was a common name for these two great peaks not only in classical times but also during the Renaissance.

Throughout the 15th century the Christian Spanish monarchs fought to expel the Muslim Moors from Spain, and when they eventually succeeded in 1492 and King Ferdinand was able to place Gibraltar under the Spanish throne, he commemorated the event heraldically by incorporating two pillars of Hercules in his royal arms, one on either side. Around the pillars he slung a ribbon with the words *Non plus ultra*, which meant both "there is nothing more beyond" (it was the end of the known world) and something like "the furthest one can go" or "the unsurpassable." But in that very same year (1492) Christopher Columbus discovered that there *was* something beyond, namely America. The Spanish kings changed the inscription *Non plus ultra* to *Plus ultra*, "there *is* something beyond" or "onward!" Instead of being the familiar utmost limit of the world the Pillars of Hercules began to be regarded as the gateway to the New World and almost a symbol of it. When the Spaniards found silver and gold in America and began to mint it, they naturally put the arms of Spain on their coins, and the arms were invariably flanked by the Pillars of Hercules. Sometimes the pillars predominated and occasionally they stood alone, but always with the ribbon slung around them.

The twin pillars left their traces. Other European states, seeking to penetrate the lucrative colonial markets, especially in the West Indies, copied the Spanish-American coins and put the two pillars with a ribbon on their own coins. Denmark, for example, did so. And in the British colonies of North America, where many kinds of coins were in circulation, the Spanish ones with the pillars were so common and popular that, instead of the currency's name, on showcards and in accounts, for example, there might be a primitive drawing of two pillars with a ribbon slung between them. When the United States established its own currency after 1776, it took the name

In a woodcut of Charles V, German Emperor and King of Spain, by Lucas Cranach, the monarch is flanked by two symbols; on one side his coat of arms with the emblems of his European possessions; on the other, two columns with a scroll that stand for his American possessions and the wealth of the New World. This symbol later became the dollar sign.

DER FORMENSCHATZ.
ART TREASURE.

1881. N⁰. 19.
LUCAS CRANACH.

L'ART PRATIQUE.
L'ARTE PRATICA.

from the German *thaler* but kept the abbreviated sign of the Spanish "pieces of eight." And so we come to the dollar sign as we know it today: an S-like device intersected by two vertical strokes, which is a simplified representation of the Pillars of Hercules with ribbon that, through the gold of South America and the kings of Spain, can be traced back to the twelve labors of Hercules in ancient Greece.

The Disarmament Badge

In February 1958 the British Campaign for Nuclear Disarmament was preparing to demonstrate by marching to the atomic center at Aldermaston. The leaders of the campaign wanted a visual symbol that would show both opponents and adherents what it stood for, and Gerald Holtom outlined various designs. He first tried something with a cross but found that the cross device had been compromised, in war decorations, for instance, and after a number of experiments he arrived at the device we all know: a vertical line with two oblique legs, the whole enclosed in a circle. If we disregard the circle, the badge is based on a simplified combination of the semaphore signals for the letters N and D, denoting Nuclear Disarmament.

A prosaic origin, to be sure. But the result was a clear and powerful emblem, easy to remember and easy to reproduce: in short, an excellent propaganda symbol. It was an immediate success and quickly spread to other countries (though not behind the Iron Curtain, where its use is banned). The actual emblem inside the circle is the same as the runic sign for R, which in the symbolism of runes is called, among other things, the "death rune" and means "death" or "the fallen." The device may be so construed, of course, but the idea was certainly not

A piece of cardboard on a pole, a modern symbol, less than 20 years old, that has been a tremendous success. Prohibited in Communist countries, the emblem is known and understood all over the world regardless of language. It stands for peace and disarmament. The picture is from Switzerland.

in Holtom's mind when he created the badge. The whole runic symbolism is a figment of the imagination, invented by German cranks at the end of the last century and the beginning of this, without the slightest foundation in the ancient use of runes. The only people who ever took it seriously were the Nazis, especially the Hitler Youth and the SS.

If a symbol has the qualities—hard to explain but easy to see—that make it popular, if in some way it is visually and psychologically "satisfying," experience shows that it will extend its range and come to symbolize more and more. The present badge originally stood only for the Campaign for Nuclear Disarmament, but in the course of a few years the use of it had spread so that it could also more or less vaguely represent general disarmament, pacifism and pacifists, and (especially in Europe) opposition to NATO and the EEC— indeed, any form of hostility to the political and economic cooperation of the western world. Worn around the neck or printed on clothes, it said something like: "I am opposed to established society and to all comfortably off people who are older than I am." The badge became to a wide extent a demonstration for "the young" against adults or "the old." But because the badge stands for "the young," it is also used by those who admire and imitate the young, especially still younger children who want to show that they are "with it," that they, too, will soon be "young."

Anne lives in Brussels. She is 11 years old and will soon be "young," like her older brothers and sisters, she thinks. That she is already "with it" she shows by writing "Peace and Love" and by drawing the peace sign in her letters.

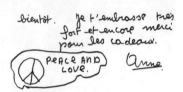

The Parting of the Ways

"To live is to choose / Oh, blessed choice / between the trivial / and the impossible." So writes the Swedish poet Karl Vennberg of the decisions we all have to make between what we think we ought to do but that can be difficult and what we all too often end up by doing.

The ancient Greeks had a story about this called "Hercules' choice." When Hercules was a youth, he went out to a lonely place in order to reflect on what he would devote his life to. There he met two women. One of them was voluptuous, provocative, and lovely; she held out every imaginable enjoyment if he would follow her. She was Pleasure, or Vice. The other woman was of noble bearing and decently attired. She was Virtue, and she explained to Hercules that nothing beautiful or good could be achieved in this world except by diligence, energy, perseverance, and courage. Hercules made his choice and followed Virtue.

The story was popular and became no less so with the advance of Christianity. Hercules seemed almost the pattern of a devout Christian denying the comfort, luxury, and temptations of "the world" in order to follow in the suffering footsteps of Jesus toward bliss and salvation. In the visual art of the Renaissance and the baroque periods the theme recurs again and again, also because it enabled the artist to paint Virtue, and perhaps Vice no less, as attractively as possible.

The idea was also expressed in quite a different way. In classical times the philosophers who called themselves Pythagoreans had come to illustrate the "parting of the ways," or choice, by means of the Greek letter upsilon, the equivalent of the capital Y of the Latin alphabet. The letter Y can be interpreted as a path that divides, and the image is even better if one arm of the Y is made wide and the other narrow. The one is the "broad path" of Vice, comfortable, easy, and without problems but leading toward materialism and perdition. The other is the "narrow path" of Virtue, steep, laborious, thorny, dangerous but at the same time morally the "right path." In European decorative art, ornamentation, and allegorical embellishment of the 16th and 17th centuries the letter Y is also sometimes seen. As a rule it symbolizes the difficult choice between virtue and vice, between evil and good, between the easy and the right path. By extension the Y can stand for the freedom of the will and man's responsibility for his own life.

Another point: why should life actually be regarded as an either/or? Could one not imagine a sort of both/and? Does a man need to betray his ideals because he likes chubby girls?

The Y representing the parting of the ways, a French Renaissance woodcut. To emphasize the symbolism, the broad path leads to judgment and punishment, with executioner's sword, lash and birch, manacles, gallows, and the stake. Those who choose, on the other hand, the narrow path are rewarded with the wreath of honor, the palms of victory, the Book of Life, the rod of sanctity, and the crown of martyrdom.

Numbers

The Magic Three

Once upon a time there were three brothers. They gave three cheers. When shall we three meet again? In proverbs and phrases, in popular speech and fairy tale, in poetry and philosophy, in propaganda and publicity, in religion and politics, almost anywhere that one looks in human life, in distant lands and remote times or today and in the Dakotas, one encounters the figure three. It is the most popular of all numbers. There is something extremely satisfying about it for body and soul; it is attractive to both the mind and the sense of rhythm. It is magic. It is sacred. It is symbolical. One time is no time. And two are so unconstant: if two agree, there will be a baby, and then there are three. And if two disagree, there has to be a mediator, and then there are three again.

Three indicates every potentiality and yet is easily compre-

In art the number three occurs again and again. It is both visually and psychologically satisfying; it is at one and the same time simple and perfect; it is not too much and nothing is lacking. *The Three Graces* by Bertel Thorvaldsen.

hended: it is probably the highest figure that can be grasped without actually counting. To the Greek philosopher Pythagoras three was the number that expressed and defined everything. It was the beginning, the middle, and the end. It stood for physical and mental health; it was the key to all and therefore a symbol of God. To Pythagoras' German successor, G.W.F. Hegel—on whom Marxism to some extent is based—all history and social existence was built up on and developed from a division into triads—thesis, antithesis, and synthesis.

In most religions the divinities are arranged in groups of three, and three of one kind or another occur again and again. There are three Graces, three Furies, three Norns, three Fates, and the number of Muses was originally three. The Bible, too, is full of threes. Noah had three sons; Abraham was visited by three angels; there was three men in the fiery furnace; Jonah spent three days and three nights in the whale's belly; "before the cock crow, thou shalt deny me thrice"; Jesus was three days in the land of the dead; there are three cardinal virtues of Christianity—faith, hope, and charity. And even when the Bible does not mention a definite number, the Christian community, or theology, requires that there should be three. This is so of the three wise men: St. Matthew says only "wise men from the East." And it is so in a way with the trinity itself: Father, Son, and Holy Ghost.

There are many other examples of this psychological need of a triad. The "liberty, equality, fraternity, or death" of the French Revolution was soon whittled down to "liberty, equality, and fraternity." Churchill's "blood, sweat, toil, and tears" is almost invariably quoted as "blood, sweat, and tears." The figure three is indispensable in all forms of rhetoric and narrative art, from the hickory-dickory-dock and the "three bags full" of nursery rhymes through the three bears, three trials, three wishes, three suitors, and three answers of fairy tales, folk ballads, and novels such as *Three Men in a Boat* and *The Three Musketeers* (though there were in fact four!)—even the Nazi chorus *Ein Volk, Ein Reich, Ein Führer.* There are three wavy lines on Royal Copenhagen porcelain, three-star brandies, and three stripes on sailor's collars. One counts to three, one has three guesses, the auctioneer's hammer falls three times—in short, we are all in innumerable ways subject to our partiality for the threefold.

The World of Four

A person who is trying to get his bearings will look first one way and then the other, both backward and forward. He will then have seen everything. The four views to the four "corners" of the world will have taken him around the horizon; and, when the ancients formed a concrete picture of the world, it seemed natural to them to divide it into four parts. This quartering of the earth and the universe made a great impression on the ancient Greeks. To them four became the "universal number." It stood for universal order as opposed to chaos and in time for all other order in nature and human life, for the creature and the Creator, for the very nature of life, indeed for life itself, for "the whole."

The confirmation of fourness was seen everywhere. Were there not four seasons, and did not human life fall clearly into four parts—childhood, youth, maturity, age? To Greek science and philosophy fours became almost compulsive: there were four elements—air, water, fire, and earth—which in various combinations formed the whole of the physical world. Men were governed by four vital principles, centered on the brain, the heart, the stomach, and the genitalia. And, corresponding to four "vital fluids," everybody could be categorized in one of four "temperaments"—choleric, melancholic, sanguine, and

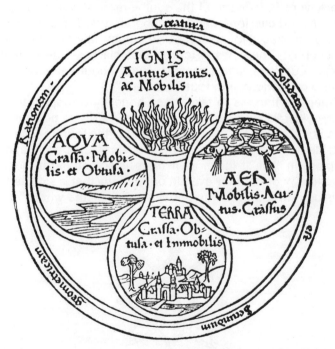

Medieval woodcut with a Latin text indicating that the universe is composed of four elements: *ignis, aqua, aer,* and *terra* (fire, water, air, and earth).

phlegmatic. There were four kinds of taste—sweet, sour, salt, and bitter; four basic emotions—anger, fear, greed, and lust; and four fundamental virtues, the "four-in-hand of the soul" — prudence, temperance, justice, and fortitude.

Most of this was taken over by Christianity, which in a remarkable way saw the quartering of the world confirmed in the Holy Gospel from the four rivers of Paradise in Genesis to the four angels at the four corners of the world that kept back the four winds of the earth. Above all, there were four gospels, four great prophets, and four archangels. Everything seemed to fit into this order of four—or was made to fit in.

When medieval history, philosophy, and social organization sought to create an overall comprehension or justice, it would often be in fours. There were four fathers of the Church, four Church "teachers," and four women saints that stood above the others—Barbara, Dorothea, Margaret, and Catherine. There were four "parts of the soul"—reason, willpower, perception, and passion—and four "liberal" arts. The universities were organized in four faculties—theology, law, medicine, and philosophy. There were four social classes—the nobility, clergy, burghers, and peasants (what about sailors?). And cities were divided into four "quarters."

When anything is to take place honestly or appeal to our sense of order and decency, fours are hardly to be avoided. This is so of the four suits of cards and of the four freedoms of President Roosevelt—from want, from fear, of speech, and of religion. In fact, it looks as if there is something in human psychology or perhaps even in our biology that is satisfied by division into four, the number symbolizing "the whole."

The Holy Seven

The number seven and the word "seven" itself play a strange part in the world of human ideas. They turn up almost everywhere: in popular idioms ("a seven-days' wonder," "in the seventh heaven" of happiness); in folklore (a broken mirror brings seven years' bad luck, a human being renews himself every seven years); in fairy tales (the seven dwarfs, seven-league boots); in book and other titles (*The Seven Lamps of Architecture, The Seventh Veil*); and in common or supposed knowledge of the world (seven seas, seven colors of the spectrum, seven notes of the scale, seven planets). It is no new phenomenon—on the contrary. The further back in time that one goes, the more sevens one comes across: the German Empire had seven electoral princes; the Middle Ages enu-

From ancient times the German emperor had been elected by the most important German princes, and in 1272 the number of these electors was fixed at seven. In this 14th-century manuscript they are identifiable by the coats of arms above. The three spiritual electors, the archbishops of Cologne, Mainz, and Trier (wearing their calottes), are followed by the four lay ones—the princes of the Palatinate, Saxony, Brandenburg, and Bohemia. In 1623 the number was increased to eight, and later to nine and ten. In 1806 the imperial crown was made hereditary, and electoral princes were abolished.

merated seven "liberal" arts; Rome was built on seven hills; the antique world had seven "wonders"; seven cities claimed to be Homer's birthplace.

In Greece, it was especially the philosophers known as the Pythagoreans who were addicted to the figure seven. Seven was for them the perfect number. Perfection itself had seven "stages," and anything that made a perfect whole had to consist of seven parts. Seemingly we can thank them for the seven notes of the scale (corresponding to the seven strings of the lyre of the god Hermes). The life of man was represented as seven "ages" (as described 2,000 years later by Shakespeare in *As You Like It*). The universe consisted of seven spheres or heavens. Corresponding to each sphere there was a note, and, when they were sounded together, the result was the "harmony of the spheres."

The seven heavens were tenacious. They play a significant part in Dante's *Divine Comedy*, c. 1336. They were accepted as a fact by Luther 200 years later. Another 200 years later the Danish author Ludvig Holberg in one of his comedies denounced them as twaddle. Yet in the 20th century we still talk of being in the "seventh heaven." The Muslims have the same idea: the Koran refers to seven heavens.

To the Christian church sevens were positively a fixed idea. And one seven bred another. Even in antiquity the Church had its list of seven cardinal virtues: the four ancient ones of prudence, temperance, justice, and fortitude plus its own additions of faith, hope, and charity. Soon the counterpart of seven deadly sins was devised, so called because they were "deadly" to the soul. Interestingly, the seven deadly sins are not deeds—such as murder, rape, blasphemy, or the like—but traits of character or states of mind: pride, wrath, envy, avarice, sloth, gluttony, and lust. But that was only a beginning. The sevens multiplied. There were the seven sacraments of the church, the seven words of Jesus on the cross, the seven stations of the *via dolorosa*, seven petitions of the Lord's Prayer, the seven joys and seven dolors of the Virgin Mary, seven good works, the seven gifts of the Holy Ghost, the seven champions of Christendom, and many more.

This thousand-year cult of the figure seven was reinforced by the connection there was thought to be between the

One of the sevens that everyone knows is that of the seven deadly sins, doubtless due to the fact that over the years the motif has appealed to an incalculable number of artists. Some of these have tried to understand the sins and to interpret them humanly, but most have wanted—or have been commissioned—to render them as abominably as possible. One of these is the German Hans Baldung Grien, whose woodcut is from 1510. On the sword of the seven sins their names are given in contemporary German as Wrath, Pride, Envy, Sloth, Gluttony, Lust, and Avarice.

groups. There were surmised mutual influences or profound interdependence between, say, the seven planets and the seven ages of man and also between the seven planets and the seven deadly sins, between the seven notes and the seven celestial spheres (as already mentioned) and the seven colors of the rainbow, between the seven cardinal virtues, the seven petitions in the Lord's Prayer, and even the seven electoral princes. There were philosophers who tried to combine all the groups of seven in one great sevenfold philosophical system.

Yet it is obvious when one considers these examples—and many more could be cited—that only in a few cases can seven be the natural or "true" number. It is possible that Rome was really built on seven hills, and it is a fact that there were (until 1623) seven electoral princes. But in the great majority of cases the number was clearly devised. Seven is not the number arrived at by counting the various things named. Seven was the starting point, the preconception and the object, the number that was wanted. A good illustration of this is the "seven colors of the spectrum": red, orange, yellow, green, blue, indigo, violet. One feels that six would have been the natural number; namely the primary colors red, yellow, and blue plus the intermediate colors orange, green, and violet. But in order that the color scale might be "perfect," it had to comprise seven colors, and so indigo was inserted between blue and violet.

That the figure seven is the main point is also indicated by the fact that these lists of seven of one thing or seven of another often started with another number—five or six or eight or nine—and were then pushed up or scaled down until the number seven was reached. And in the cases where there have always been seven (the seven wonders of the ancient world, for example), the lists have varied. The subjects are not always the same. But the number is! The figure seven is more important than what forms it. That at any rate is the impression one gets when reading Revelation. We are told of seven letters to seven churches, of seven spirits, seven candlesticks, seven stars, seven angels, the seven-sealed book, the seven-headed dragon with seven crowns, seven eyes, seven trumpets, the seven-horned beast, the seven plagues, seven cups, seven mountains, seven vessels, etc. We also meet with the sevens elsewhere in the New Testament: for example, in the genealogy of Jesus

and in connection with his miracles. He drives out seven
spirits; he feeds the multitude with seven fishes.

But the New Testament's preoccupation with the figure
seven is easily outstripped by the Old Testament. This work is
so shot through with sevens that to enumerate them is quite
outside the scope of this book. God ended his work on the
seventh day; Noah stayed "other seven days"; Jacob served
seven years for Leah and seven years for Rachel; Samson had
seven locks on his head; Job's friends sat down with him seven

Perhaps the most important of all the sevens that occur so frequently in the
Old Testament is the seven-branched candlestick, the Menorah, which is fully
described in chapter 25 of the Book of Exodus. It was and still is the
central Jewish symbol, and despite the prohibition against images in the
Ten Commandments it was frequently depicted even in ancient times. The
example shown here is a mosaic from the 6th century in a synagogue at
Huldah in Palestine. In 1949 the state of Israel placed the seven-branched
candlestick in its national arms.

days and seven nights; rewards are sevenfold and vengeance is sevenfold or perhaps seven times sevenfold. Sometimes it becomes almost an obsession: Pharaoh's dream of seven fat and seven lean kine; the seven good and seven thin ears of corn, which meant seven years of plenty and seven years of famine. Or, in the account of the fall of Jericho: seven priests bearing seven rams' horns before the host, "and the seventh day ye shall compass the city seven times . . . " The feast of the tabernacle lasted seven days, as did the feast of unleavened bread. There were seven archangels (the Christians have three or four) and seven times for prayer. Invocations were seven and maledictions seven. So magical and sacred was seven that the Hebrew word for "oath" stems from the word for "seven." To swear was "to say seven." But first and foremost, of course, the Creation had taken seven days. "And on the seventh day God ended his work which he had made; and he rested on the seventh day." We now approach the explanation of it all: the division of time into what we call "a week," comprising seven days.

In primitive religions the moon is usually more significant than the sun. It was regarded as far more influential and was worshipped as a god millennia before anyone paid any similar attention to the sun. This ancient priority in the conception of the world and the universe can perhaps be illustrated by an old schoolboy joke: the moon is much more useful than the sun because it shines at night when it is dark, whereas the sun shines by day when it is light.

The real point, undoubtedly, was that the moon is far easier to observe and that its appearance and form vary in a way that constitutes one of the most conspicuous natural phenomena. Observation of the phases of the moon may have been man's first science. At any rate it is the first point of departure for any chronology. From new moon to new moon is just over 29 days, and this means that the four phases of the moon—from new moon to half-moon (waxing), from half-moon to full moon, from full moon to half-moon (waning), and from half-moon to new moon—each lasts about seven days. This calculation is at least 6,000 years old, perhaps much more, and the cycle of four times seven days had a great impact on the people who made it. It was probably a contributory factor that the period of female

The Swedish saint Bridget with her sevenfold crown, expressive of God's sevenfold grace (as seen in a vision by a monk in one of the monasteries she founded). Painting, c. 1490, on a triptych, National Historical Museum, Stockholm.

menstruation is also about 28 days (and indeed there is a connection). Fertilization, procreation, birth, and life were clearly linked to these four times seven days. The week of seven days and the four weeks that made a "lunar" month formed the earliest calendar. Thousands of years later, when time began to be calculated according to the sun, lunar reckoning was dropped, and the months lenghtened in order that twelve of them might fit the 365 days of the solar year. The Muslims, however, still use a lunar calendar, and there are remnants of it in Christian chronology. For example, Easter is calculated as the first Sunday after the first full moon after the spring equinox.

The people who wrote the Old Testament inherited a good deal of their conceptions from the Babylonians, and the Babylonians were to a quite incredible degree dominated by the idea of seven. They were the first to divide the days of their life into periods of seven, each period of seven ending (or beginning) with a holy day. It was the one the Jews took over as the "sabbath," a word which means "fullness." To the Babylonians the word "seven" meant the same thing. "Seven-ness" was the same as "the whole," the world, the universe, eternity. "Seven" was a term for divine authority and power, used in incantations and divine services in magic and in religion. "Seven" brought good luck, and merely to say it acted as a protection. To do something seven times gave strength and moral purification.

Besides the purely lunar aspect there are one or two other factors that may have contributed to the high esteem of the figure seven. Seven is the sum of three plus four, and both of these figures are magic and sacred. Three is "God's number," occurring again and again in religious concepts, in myths, and in magic rites. Four is the "world number": in the physical world there were—or were invented—fours everywhere—four corners of the world, four phases of the moon, four elements, four temperaments. There is much to suggest that the number seven in many cases was regarded as a "deliberate" result of three plus four, as God plus the world, as the spiritual forces of the universe plus the physical, combined in a unity that therefore was unsurpassably strong. The division into three "of spirit" and four of "the world" recurs in many of the later groupings of seven. The seven cardinal virtues consist of four practical and three theological ones. Of the seven electoral princes, three were princes of the church and four were temporal rulers. Of the seven petitions of the Lord's Prayer, three are about God and four about fellow man. And so on.

Conducive to all this may have been the fact that the figure seven in Babylon (and elsewhere) formed a very important part of practical calculating. A square with a side of seven is twice as large as a square with a side of five and in turn is half as large as one with a side of ten, which in turn is half as large as a square with a side of twice seven. The four areas of squares cited are: 25, 49 (nearly 50), 100, and 196 (nearly 200). The inaccuracy was so slight that this 5-7-10-14 system was infinitely useful in day-to-day application in calculating surfaces and measuring land: for example, in agriculture, engineering, partitioning, irrigation. Seven is thus an essential figure in a calculating system that is otherwise based on the number ten.

Finally, there are those who think that the special position of the figure seven has something to do with the fact that it could *not* be applied to anything at all. It does not fit into the series 2-4-8, nor into 3-6-9-12 or 5-10-20. It cannot be equally divided; it is outside the system, something special. It stands by itself.

To return to the week! In time each of the days in the seven-day period became attached to one of the seven "celestial orbs" by which the Babylonians believed themselves to be influenced: the sun, the moon, and the five planets (all that were known in those days), often called together "the seven planets." The seven days, following each other in regular succession, were called the sun's day, the moon's day, and so forth; and, when the Babylonian chronology and the seven-day week spread to Greece and later to the Roman Empire, they translated the Babylonian names of the planets into their own (which were at the same time names of divinities). Thus we have Sun's Day (Sunday), Moon's Day (Monday), Mars' Day (French *mardi*), Mercury's Day (*mercredi*), Jove's day (*jeudi*), Venus's Day (*vendredi*), and Saturn's Day (Saturday). The Germanic peoples, including the Anglo-Saxons and Scandinavians, adopted the seven-day week from the Romans in pagan times but renamed four of the days, calling them by the names of the corresponding Norse gods: Tuesday (from Tir), Wednesday (from Woten), Thursday (from Thor), and Friday (from Freya).

As may be imagined, the Church opposed these pagan names, both the Roman and the later Germanic ones, and sought to have them abolished. In the year 200 the churchman Tertullian suggested the names "First Day," "Second Day," etc., and this idea was revived in the Middle Ages. But unsuccessfully. The Orthodox Church of Byzantium urged "Apostle's Day" in place of "Thursday" and "God's Mother's Day" for Friday. It was all of no use. In 1620 an Italian cleric recommended naming the seven days after the seven sacraments (and the twelve months after the twelve apostles). No more came of this proposal than of the earlier ones. All that the Church has to show for over a thousand years of campaigning against the un-Christian names for the days is the replacement of "Sunday" in some Latin countries by "Lord's Day" (French *dimanche*, Spanish *domingo*). In 1793 the French revolutionaries abolished the seven-day week and introduced a new, revolutionary week of ten days. It was not a success, if for no other reason than perhaps because it reduced the annual number of "Sundays" from 52 to 36. After some ten years of desperate attempts to keep the ten-day week alive Napoleon saw that the old system was too strong and in 1805 reverted to the seven-day week: a quarter of the time between new moon and new moon, the mysterious seven-day period of the moon's phases.

Index